FIRST BOOK OF BRIDGE

SUMMARY OF POINT-COUNT BIDDING

OPENING BIDS

Points	*Bid*
12 or 13, with good suit	1 of suit
14, with any suit	1 of suit
16 to 18, with stoppers	1 NT
22 to 24, with stoppers	2 NT
25 to 27, with stoppers	3 NT
25 or more, with good suit	2 of suit

RESPONSES TO 1 OF SUIT

6 to 16	1 of new suit
9 to 16	2 of lower suit
17 or more	Jump in new suit
6 to 10, with trump support	Raise to 2
13 to 16	Raise to 3
8 or less, with trumps and void or singleton	Raise to 4
6 to 9	1 NT
13 to 15, with stoppers	2 NT
16 or 17, with stoppers	3 NT

POINT COUNT

Ace	4
King	3
Queen	2
Jack	1

SUMMARY OF POINT-COUNT BIDDING

RESPONSES TO 2 OF SUIT

5 or less	2 NT
6 or more	Positive response

RESPONSES TO 1 NT

0 to 7	Pass or 2 of long suit
8 or 9	2 NT
10 to 15	3 NT or 3 of long suit
16 or more	Aim for slam

RESPONSES TO 2 NT

0 to 3	Pass
4 to 10	Bid game
11 or more	Aim for slam

REBIDS BY OPENER

13 to 16	Minimum or pass
17 to 19	Invite a game
20 or more	Force to game

REBIDS BY RESPONDER

6 to 9	Minimum or pass
10 to 12	Invite game
13 or more	Force to game

KEY NUMBERS

Game	26 points
Small Slam	33 points
Grand Slam	37 points

EVERYDAY HANDBOOKS

FIRST BOOK
OF BRIDGE

ALFRED SHEINWOLD

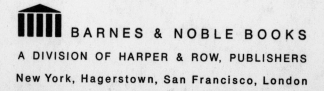 BARNES & NOBLE BOOKS

A DIVISION OF HARPER & ROW, PUBLISHERS

New York, Hagerstown, San Francisco, London

This book was originally published by Sterling Publishing Co., Inc. It is here reprinted by special arrangement.

Copyright 1952 by Sterling Publishing Co., Inc. All rights reserved under International and Pan-American Copyright Conventions. Printed in the United States of America. No part of this book may be used or reproduced in any manner without written permission except in the case of brief quotations embodied in critical articles and reviews. For information address Harper & Row, Publishers, Inc., 10 East 53d Street, New York, N.Y. 10022. Published simultaneously in Canada by Fitzhenry & Whiteside Limited, Toronto.

ISBN: 0 −06 −463242 −8

87 88 89 90   20 19 18 17 16

Table of Contents

GLOSSARY

AUCTION: the bidding.

BALANCED (a balanced hand, balanced distribution): including no void suit, no singleton, and not more than one doubleton.

BID: an offer to take a definite number of tricks at a named suit or at notrump.

BIDDABLE (biddable suit, biddable hand): strong enough for a bid.

BLACKWOOD: a method of asking partner how many aces and kings he holds; used for slam bidding only.

BLOCK: to win a trick in the wrong hand with the result that you cannot continue to play a long suit.

BOOK: the first six tricks for declarer.

BONUS: a score written above the line.

CASH: to take a sure trick at once rather than later on.

CLUB: one of the four suits—♣.

CONTRACT: the final bid.

CROSSRUFF: a series of tricks in which declarer trumps one suit in his own hand and another suit in the dummy.

CUT: to remove part of the deck and put the bottom portion on top of the removed portion.

DECK: the standard fifty-two cards.

DECLARER: the player of the team with the winning bid who was first to name the suit (or notrump) and who plays the hand.

DEFENDER: either of the two partners who play against declarer.

DEUCE: the two-spot of any suit.

DIAMOND: one of the four suits —♦.

DISCARD: to play a card of a suit (not the trump suit) that is different from the suit led.

DISTRIBUTION: shape; the pattern formed by the number of cards you hold in the four suits—as, 4-3-3-3 or 6-4-2-1, etc.

DOUBLE: an attempt to increase penalties when you think an opponent's bid will be defeated.

DOUBLETON: a holding of only two cards in a suit.

DRAW TRUMPS: to lead the trump suit until the defenders have no more trumps left.

DROP: to capture an opponent's high card by playing a higher card of your own, on which his must fall.

DUMMY: declarer's partner; also, the hand of declarer's partner.

ENTRY: a card that can win a trick and thus provide the right to lead on the next trick.

ESTABLISH: to promote low cards to winning rank.

FINESSE: an attempt to win a trick with a card that is not the highest playable card of its suit.

FORCING BID: a bid that your partner is supposed to respond to.

FREE BID: a response or rebid made immediately after an opponent's bid.

GAME: 100 points or more scored below the line.

GRAND SLAM: a bid for all thirteen tricks; a bid of "seven."

HEART: one of the four suits—♥.

HIGH-LOW: a method of signalling (by playing first high and then low) used by the defenders to show strength or to ask that a suit be led again.

HONORS: the five highest cards of a suit—particularly of the trump suit (if any). At notrump only, the four aces.

INTERMEDIATES: high spot cards, such as tens, nines, and eights.

JUMP BID: a bid of more than necessary to outrank the previous bid.

MAJOR SUIT: spades or hearts.

MINOR SUIT: diamonds or clubs.

NON-VULNERABLE: said of a side that has not yet scored a game in the rubber being played.

NOTRUMP: a type of bid specifying that there will be no trump suit.

ONE-OVER-ONE: a response or rebid in a new suit at the level of one (e.g. 1 ♥ in response to 1 ♦).

OPENING BID: the first bid of any auction.

OVERCALL: a bid made by the side that has not opened the bidding.

OVERTRICK: a trick in excess of the contract.

PART SCORE: a contract of less than game.

PASS: a statement that you make during the auction when you don't wish to bid, double, or redouble.

PENALTY DOUBLE: a double made when you expect to collect penalties, as distinguished from the *takeout* double.

PRE-EMPTIVE BID: a high bid intended to keep the opponents out of the auction.

PROMOTE: to bring cards nearer to winning rank by playing two or more higher cards on the same trick.

RAISE: a bid for more tricks in a suit (or notrump) first named by your partner.

REBIDDABLE: strong enough for another bid.

REDOUBLE: an attempt to increase bonuses when an opponent had doubled your side at a bid that you think can be made.

RESPONSE: a bid made in answer to your partner's opening bid.

RUBBER: a series of hands that ends when either side scores two games.

RUFF: to play a trump on a side suit when you cannot follow suit.

SACRIFICE BID: a deliberate over-bid.

SEQUENCE: two or more cards in unbroken order of rank, e.g. K-Q-J, or Q-J, etc.

SET: to defeat a contract.

SET UP: to promote low cards to winning rank (same as to establish).

SHAPE: the distribution of your hand; the pattern formed by the number of cards you have in the four suits.

SHUT-OUT BID: a high bid intended to keep the opponents out of the auction.

SIDE SUIT: any suit except trump.

SINGLETON: a holding of only one card in a suit.

SLAM: a contract for twelve or thirteen tricks.

SLUFF: to discard.

SMALL SLAM: a bid for twelve of the thirteen tricks; a bid of "six."

SPADE: one of the four suits—♠.

SPOT CARD: any card lower than the jack.

STOPPER: a card that will sooner or later take a trick in a suit.

SUIT: the thirteen cards that all bear the same symbol (♠, ♥, ♦, or ♣).

TABLE: the dummy hand (which is spread on the table).

TAKEOUT: a response in a new suit.

TAKEOUT DOUBLE: a double that asks your partner to name his best suit.

TREY: the three-spot of any suit.

TRICK: four cards, one from each player's hand.

TRUMP: to play a trump card on a suit in which you are void.

TRUMP SUIT: the suit named in the final contract.

TRUMP SUPPORT: a holding of enough trumps to raise partner's suit.

TWO-OVER-ONE: a response at the level of two in a suit of lower rank than the suit named in your partner's opening bid.

UNBALANCED DISTRIBUTION: a holding of a void suit, a singleton, or more than one doubleton.

VOID SUIT: a holding of no cards in a suit.

VULNERABLE: said of a side that has scored one game towards the rubber being played.

1. How To Begin

Contract Bridge is the finest and also the most popular of all card games. You will find that a knowledge of the game helps you make friends and provides you with a common interest. Almost everyone at one time or another plays bridge, so the ability to play the game may well serve, later on, as an introduction to people whom you want to meet.

Bridge is not, however, just a way to make friends. People play it because they like it. You will like it also, and you will find it more enjoyable to play well than to play poorly.

Fortunately, it isn't hard to learn how to play contract bridge well. If you read this book with thought and attention, you'll get a very sound idea of the game and it won't take you long to become a good player. However you read it, enough will stick in your memory to give you a workable idea of the game.

Of course, you will also need to practice by playing. First, there's no advantage in reading about a game if you aren't going to play it. Secondly, the more you play the easier you will remember the right things to do. Finally, you'll *enjoy* playing bridge; and this is the most important reason for playing any game.

You've probably seen people playing bridge, and if so you'll know how to go through the motions even if you don't know the reasons for those motions. If you've never watched the game, do so. Certain actions (take shuffling the cards, for instance) are hard to explain in words, but are very easily understood if you see them being carried out.

The next couple of pages are an explanation of things you probably know already. If you've ever watched bridge being played, skim through them lightly. However, if you have no chance of watching a bridge game, read the next few pages carefully.

EQUIPMENT: You need four people, two decks of cards with jokers removed (one deck will do in a pinch), a piece of paper and a pencil. It's handy to have a table and four chairs, but real enthusiasts will play bridge on almost anything!

PARTNERS: The players who sit across the table from each other are partners. North and South are partners. They play against East and West, who are also partners. (See p. 20.)

THE DRAW: The players draw cards to select the first dealer. The deck is spread out face down, and each player draws one card. The player who draws the highest card is the first dealer. Sometimes partners are selected in the same way, so that the two players who draw the *two* highest cards become partners against the other two.

THE CUT: The first dealer takes one of the two decks, shuffles it, and puts it near the player at his right for a cut. The player cuts the cards by lifting some cards from the top of the deck and placing them nearer to the dealer. The dealer completes the cut by lifting the uncut cards (those that are farther away from him) and placing them on top of the cards that are nearer to him. The cards *must* be cut for every deal.

THE DEAL: The dealer then proceeds to hand out the cards one at a time, face down, beginning with the player at his left and continuing from left to right (like the hands of a clock). There are fifty-two cards in the deck, and at the end of a deal each player has received thirteen of them.

Nobody touches the cards while they are being dealt. The

cards are allowed to form in four little piles on the table. When the dealer gives the last card of the deck to himself, all four players are ready to pick up their hands at the same time.

After the first deal has been played out, the deal passes around to the next player to the left. For example, if South deals the first hand, West will deal the second, North will deal the third, and East will deal the fourth. This brings us back to South for the fifth hand, and so on.

SHUFFLING: During all of the business of cutting and dealing, the dealer's partner is busy shuffling the second deck. When he has shuffled it carefully, he puts it *at his right* in the corner of the table. That leaves a shuffled deck where it can be picked up by the next dealer.

ASSORTING YOUR HAND: As soon as the last card has been dealt, but not before, each player picks up his cards and assorts them. The best way to assort your hand is to separate it into suits, with the red and black suits alternating. Within each suit, put the higher cards at the left and the lower cards at the right.

The cards rank in each suit as follows: Ace (highest)-king-queen-jack-10-9-8-7-6-5-4-3-2 (lowest).

THE BIDDING: The dealer speaks first, and he may bid or pass. Let's not worry for the moment about what a bid means. Let's just observe that each player speaks in turn, going around to the left in the same way that the cards were dealt. Eventually, a bid will be followed by a pass from each of the other three players; and that will end the bidding. That last bid, followed by three passes, is called "the contract."

(If the dealer passes and the other three players also pass, the hand is "passed out" and the deal goes to the next player.)

DECLARER AND DUMMY: In the bidding of any hand, some player makes the highest bid. That player's side is the *declaring* side; and the opponents are the *defending* side.

Each bid consists of a number and one other word, which is either the name of a suit or "notrump." The player of the declaring side who *first* mentioned the suit or notrump named in the final bid is called "the declarer." (He is sometimes but not always, the player who has made the highest bid.)

Declarer's partner is called the dummy, because he just sits still (like a ventriloquist's dummy) during the play of a hand. His hand is also called the dummy.

THE OPENING LEAD: When the bidding has ended, the player at declarer's left makes the opening lead. To do so, he selects a card from his hand and places it face up in the middle of the table.

EXPOSING THE DUMMY: As soon as the opening lead has been made, but not before, declarer's partner puts his entire hand face up on the table. He arranges the cards in four slanted piles, one pile for each suit, pointing lengthwise towards his partner. The trumps (if there is a trump suit) must be at his right (which is declarer's left).

You will sometimes see inexperienced players put down their trumps when they are dummy before the opening lead has been made. This is unnecessary and foolish. You will never see this done by a good player. After placing his cards on the table, the dummy sits still and takes a quiet interest in the proceedings until the last card has been played.

THE FIRST TRICK: Declarer looks at the dummy and selects a card from the dummy to place in the middle of the table, together with the card which was the opening lead. Next, the leader's partner takes one card from his own hand and places it in the middle of the table. Finally, the declarer takes one card from his own hand and places it in the middle of the table.

Those four cards in the middle of the table are called a *trick*. As soon as they have been played and taken by the side that won the trick, the trick ends and a new trick begins with the play of four different cards. There are thirteen tricks in the play of every hand, as you can see by dividing 52 by 4.

LATER TRICKS: The first card of any trick is called a lead. The player who wins the first trick leads a card for the second trick. The winner of the second trick leads for the third trick, and so on. This process continues until all thirteen tricks have been played.

When declarer wins a trick, either in his own hand or in the dummy, he picks up the four cards, arranges them in a neat pile, and places them face down at the edge of the table nearest to him.

One defender, likewise, keeps all the tricks won by his side. By custom, these tricks are kept by the partner of the player whose card wins the first defensive trick.

Each side should keep its tricks face down and crisscrossed or overlapped in such a way that any player can tell at a glance how many tricks are in the pile.

FOLLOWING SUIT: At each trick, each player in turn is required to play a card of the same suit as the card led. For example, if the lead is a spade, each of the remaining players must play a spade if he can do so. This is called "following suit."

DISCARDING: When you cannot follow suit (because you do not have any card in the suit led), you may play a card of any suit. Such a play is called a "discard."

TRUMPING OR RUFFING: When a suit is named in the final bid, that is the "trump suit," and each of the thirteen cards of that suit is called a "trump." When a player leads a "side suit" (not a trump), and you cannot follow suit, you may play a trump. Such an act is called "trumping" or "ruffing."

WINNING A TRICK: When a trick includes one or more trumps, it is won by the highest trump in the trick. A trick that does not contain a trump is won by the highest card of the suit led.

For example, suppose that spades are trumps. West leads the queen of hearts, and the seven of diamonds is played from dummy (dummy has no hearts). East "follows suit" with the eight of hearts, and South plays the deuce of spades (he has no hearts either). The trick is won by the deuce of spades, the only trump included in the trick.

Note that the seven of diamonds is merely a discard. It could not possibly win the trick, since it is neither a trump nor a card of the suit led. Note also that *any* trump, even the deuce, wins a trick from any non-trump.

When the final contract is in "notrump," this means that there is *no trump suit*. At a notrump contract a trick is always won by the highest card of the suit led.

SCORING: When all thirteen tricks have been played, it is possible to write down a score for that hand. The scorepad should be kept in a corner of the table in full view at all times. Two scores may be kept—one by each side.

There is more to know about scoring, but that will come in a little while. We must first find out what bidding really means.

THE STRUCTURE OF CONTRACT BRIDGE

In any game of bridge two main activities take place: bidding and playing. The bidding is a sort of prediction of what will happen in the play of the cards. Or, to put it another way, you make promises during the bidding and you are supposed to fulfill them during the play.

Let's see how this works with an example. In the diagram below, North and South are partners, playing against the partnership of East and West.

North

West   East

South

Whenever North speaks up during the bidding, his bid is equally binding on South and vice versa. The same holds true for East and West. The principle is that the partners stand or fall together on everything they say or do.

It cannot be overstressed that contract bridge is a partnership game. You will get good results, and you will enjoy the game, if you work *with* your partner rather than *against* him.

Have you ever attended an auction sale? Everybody offers to buy the object being sold, and the person who makes the highest offer (or "bid") has bought that object. This is very much what happens in the bidding of contract bridge. Each player in turn has the chance to bid higher than the previous bid, and the player who makes the highest bid thereby wins the contract.

Contract bridge is played for points, and the auction is an attempt to win those points. This doesn't mean that you try to score up to some definite goal, for example up to a hundred or a thousand points. You just go along, trying to score as many points as possible. Whenever you stop playing, the score is added up, and the side with the higher score wins.

In your attempt to win points you aim at a few familiar targets. The easiest way to score points is to win "rubbers." Another good way is to bid and make "slams." A third way is to collect penalties from the opponents when they bid too ambitiously.

A "rubber" consists of two "games" out of three. You may, however, win the first two games, and then you don't bother to play the third.

As a general rule you must bid fairly high to score a game: nine tricks at notrump; ten tricks at spades or hearts; eleven tricks at clubs or diamonds. Incidentally, this important difference between ten and eleven tricks is the reason spades and hearts are called the "major" suits while diamonds and clubs are called the "minor" suits.

Your aim in bidding is to predict as accurately as possible the number of tricks you can win in the play of the cards. It doesn't pay to bid only enough to become declarer. Bid for as many tricks as you think your side can make. This will often be *much* higher than any previous bid. *You get credit towards game only for what you have bid*—regardless of how many "extra" tricks you may win.

THE MEANING OF BIDS

The number of tricks mentioned in your bid is not actually the number of tricks that you are supposed to win. The first six tricks are called "the book." Your bid indicates the number of tricks that you hope to win *in addition* to those first six.

For example, a bid of "one spade" means that you hope to win seven (six plus one) tricks if spades are trumps. A bid of "three notrump" means that you hope to win nine (six plus three) tricks with no trump suit at all. A bid of "seven hearts" means that you hope to win all thirteen tricks with hearts as trumps.

DOUBLES AND REDOUBLES

At your turn to bid you may "double" the previous bid, provided it was made by an opponent. Your double means: "Opponents, I think that you cannot fulfill this contract. Therefore I want to increase the amount of the penalty that you will suffer."

Naturally you cannot double your partner, but only an opponent. Note also that you can double only the last bid that has been made before your turn to bid. You can't double a bid that has already been cancelled out by some higher bid.

When you double an opponent, you stand to gain if you are a good prophet, but you will lose points if there is no further bidding and the opponent makes his contract after all. For making a doubled contract, your opponent scores more points than if he had simply made his contract undoubled. (The word "double" is not exact in this connection, because the amount of gain or loss is not actually multiplied by two, but sometimes is greater.)

If your opponent thinks that you are a very bad prophet he may say "redouble" after you have doubled. If he succeeds in making his contract, his gain will be greatly increased because of his redouble. However, in the event that he fails to make his contract after redoubling, his losses (and your gains) will be increased.

THE RANK OF SUITS

Whenever you bid, you *must* bid higher than any previous bid. This may be done in either of two ways:

(a) by bidding for a larger number of tricks
(b) by bidding for the same number of tricks in a higher suit (or notrump)

The first way is, of course, easy. Any bid of two is higher than any bid of one; any bid of three is higher than any bid of two; and so on.

The second way is likewise easy when you know how the suits rank:

NOTRUMP (*highest*)

SPADES

HEARTS

DIAMONDS

CLUBS (*lowest*)

A bid of one club is the lowest possible bid. If another player bids one club, you may then bid one diamond. A bid of one heart would be higher still, and one spade would outbid one heart. A bid of one notrump is the highest bid at the one-level.

If you want to outbid one notrump you must say two (or more) of some suit. It is also possible to make a higher bid in the *same* suit by merely increasing the number of tricks mentioned in the bid. For example, your partner might bid one notrump, and you might then say three notrump; or he might say two spades and you might jump all the way to six spades; and so on.

SCORING

A scorepad has a line up and down the middle. In the left-hand half you write the scores made by your side; in the right-hand half you write the scores made by the opponents. These two halves of the scorepad are often labeled "We" and "They."

Another line runs across the pad. This makes it possible for you to write some scores "above the line" and other scores "below the line."

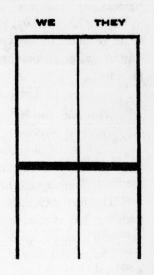

BELOW THE LINE: You score below the line only for a contract that you have bid and made. You never score below the line when an opponent is declarer; and nobody can score below the line when the declarer fails to make his contract.

The score that you write below the line when a contract is bid and made is the number of tricks mentioned in the bid multiplied by the trick value of the suit (or notrump) mentioned in the bid.

TRICK VALUES

Spades: 30 points per trick
Hearts: 30 points per trick
Diamonds: 20 points per trick
Clubs: 20 points per trick
Notrump: 40 points for the first trick; 30 points for each later trick.

Suppose you bid and make three clubs. Clubs count 20 points per trick. You therefore multiply 3 × 20 and write down 60 points below the line.

Your score below the line would be 90 points if you had bid and made three spades, because spades are worth 30 points per trick. Your score would be 100 points if you had bid and made three notrump, because the value of notrump is 40 points for the first trick and 30 points for each remaining trick.

AFTER A DOUBLE

Spades or Hearts } 60 points per trick

Diamonds or Clubs } 40 points per trick

Notrump: 80 points for the first trick; 60 points for each later trick.

When your contract is *doubled*, the trick value is multiplied by two. For example, if you make a doubled contract of two spades, your score below the line is 120 points since each of the two tricks is worth 60 points.

AFTER A REDOUBLE

Spades or Hearts } 120 points per trick

Diamonds or Clubs } 80 points per trick

Notrump: 160 points for the first trick; 120 points for each later trick

When your contract is *doubled and redoubled*, the trick value is multiplied by four (twice the doubled value). For example, if you make a redoubled contract of two spades, your score below the line is 240 points since each of the tricks is worth 120 points.

A GAME: Whenever your score below the line is 100 points or more, you draw a line across the pad underneath that score. This line indicates that a "game" has been ended, so that both sides must now start afresh to work towards the next game.

You score no points for winning a single game, but a side that wins two games out of three wins the "rubber." If you win the first two games, you don't bother to play the third game, but you end that rubber immediately.

Your bonus for winning the rubber will go above the line, but this bonus is the result of what happens below the line! Always remember that the only thing you ever write below the line is the value of *tricks bid and made*.

ABOVE THE LINE: There are many different reasons for writing a score above the line. Let's mention them all, and then we can examine each kind of score more closely. You score above the line for extra tricks, "honors," bonus for making a doubled contract, bonus for a slam, bonus for the rubber, penalties for defeating the opponents, and bonus for extra tricks when doubled.

EXTRA TRICKS: You will sometimes win one or two tricks more than your contract calls for, and these tricks are called "extra" tricks or overtricks. Extra tricks are scored *above the line,* at the usual trick value. For example, if you bid three spades and win ten tricks, you score 90 points below the line (for the first nine tricks, as called for by your contract) and 30 points above the line (for the extra trick).

HONORS: The five highest cards are called "honors": ace, king, queen, jack, ten. When the hand is played at a trump suit, a player who has *in his own hand* four of the five best trumps (A-K-Q-J, or A-K-Q-10, or A-K-J-10, or A-Q-J-10, or K-Q-J-10) scores a bonus of 100 points for his side. (It is usually the declarer or dummy who holds the honors, but even a defender may hold them and get credit for them.)

When you hold all five of the best trumps (A-K-Q-J-10) in one hand you get a bonus of 150 points (instead of only 100 points).

At a notrump contract the aces are the honors, and you score a bonus only when you hold all four aces in one hand. The bonus for honors at notrump is 150 points.

MAKING A DOUBLED CONTRACT: You score a bonus of 50 points if you make a doubled or a redoubled contract. The amount of this bonus never changes; it is always just 50 points.

VULNERABLE AND NON-VULNERABLE SCORES: Some scores depend on whether or not you are "vulnerable." This word (which means, literally, "capable of being wounded") is applied to you when you have already won one game of a rubber. When both sides have won a game, both sides are vulnerable. When only one side has won a game, that side is vulnerable, and the other side is "non-vulnerable."

SLAM BONUSES: You score a bonus for a slam only when you bid it and make it. A "grand slam" is a bid of seven, a contract that calls for all thirteen tricks. A "small slam" is a bid of six, a contract that calls for twelve of the thirteen tricks.

BONUS

	Non-Vulnerable	Vulnerable
SMALL SLAM	500 points	750 points
GRAND SLAM	1000 points	1500 points

These bonuses are never changed by anything but the vulnerability of the side that bids the slam. (The vulnerability of the other side doesn't matter.)

RUBBER BONUS: You get a bonus of 700 points if you win the rubber before the opponents have managed to win a game. If the opponents have managed to win a game at any time during the rubber, your bonus for winning the rubber is only 500 points.

PENALTIES: When a declarer fails to make a contract, the *opponents* score above the line. The amount of that score, sometimes called a "penalty for undertricks," depends on declarer's vulnerability and whether or not the contract was doubled (or redoubled).

When your contract has not been doubled, the penalty for being set is 50 points per trick if you are not vulnerable. It would be 100 points per trick if you were vulnerable. These penalties "per trick" apply only to the tricks by which you fall short of your contract. For example, if you are defeated by one trick not vulnerable, the penalty is 50 points; if you are set two tricks, the penalty is 100 points, and so on.

When your contract has been doubled the penalties are much steeper. Not vulnerable, the penalty is 100 points for the first undertrick; 200 points for each additional undertrick. Thus, the penalty would be 300 points for a two-trick defeat; 500 points, for a three-trick defeat; and so on. Vulnerable, the penalty would be 200 points for the first undertrick; 300 points for each additional undertrick.

The penalty for undertricks when the contract has been redoubled is exactly twice the doubled value. Not vulnerable, 200 points for the first trick, 400 points for each later trick; vulnerable, 400 points for the first trick, and 600 points for each later trick.

BONUS FOR OVERTRICKS WHEN DOUBLED: As we have seen, there is a bonus for making your contract when an opponent has *doubled* you. There is an additional bonus if you succeed in making not only your contract but also additional tricks or "overtricks."

If you are not vulnerable, you score 100 points for each such overtrick; if vulnerable, 200 points.

A redouble makes these tricks twice as valuable: 200 points per overtrick when you are non-vulnerable; 400 points, vulnerable.

Look at the diagram at the side of this explanation. You will see a typical scorepad with only two figures on it.

"We" have just played a hand at a contract of two spades, making three. We score 60 points below the line for the tricks bid and made, and 30 points above the line for the extra trick.

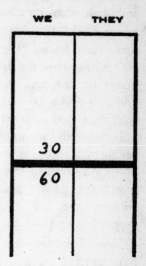

Note that each score is written as near as possible to the horizontal line. Later scores will work upwards and downwards from that line.

Now we see the same scorepad after the end of the second hand. This time "They" have played the hand at a contract of two notrump, making four.

"They" score 70 points below the line for the two tricks bid and made (40 points for the first trick at notrump, and 30 points for each later trick). The two extra tricks, at 30 points each, are scored above the line.

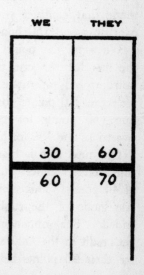

Here's the same scorepad after the end of the third hand. "They" got a little too ambitious when they bid three hearts. "We" doubled and set them three tricks. "We" score 500 points above the line: 100 points for the first undertrick and 200 points for each of the remaining two undertricks.

Incidentally, we must avoid licking our chops as we write down this excellent score. One good score doesn't make us a winner, and it's considered unsporting to gloat anyway.

Now we have the fourth hand entered on the scorepad. "We" bid one notrump and made that contract with two overtricks and 150 honors.

We score 40 points below the line for the one trick at notrump bid and made. Then we score 210 points above the line (60 points for the two overtricks and 150 for honors).

Our next step is to draw a line across, under our score of 40 points. This shows that one game of the rubber has ended. The opponents will get credit in the final addition for their 70 points below the line, but they can no longer use that score to count towards game. Bridge players say that the score of the opponents is "wiped out."

WE	THEY
500	
30	60
60	70

WE	THEY
210	
500	
30	60
60	70
40	

On the fifth hand of the rubber the opponents bid three clubs and just made it.

They score 60 points below the line: 20 points per trick for clubs.

Note that this is written under the new horizontal line that we drew after the fourth hand. It is the first hand in the struggle for a new game, and their previous score of 70 points below the line does not help them.

The sixth hand of the rubber was a very bad one for us. The opponents bid one spade, we doubled, and they redoubled. The declarer made eight tricks—one more than he needed for his contract.

They score 120 points below the line, because the redoubled value of the tricks at spades is 120 points per trick. Since this is enough for a game (even without the 60 points scored previously), we sadly draw another line under the figure 120. But that isn't all!

Above the line, they score 250 points: 50 points for making the contract, and 200 points for making an overtrick redoubled.

WE	THEY
210	
500	
30	60
60	70
40	
	60

WE	THEY
210	
500	250
30	60
60	70
40	
	60
	120

The seventh hand ends the rubber. The opponents bid six spades (a small slam) and make that contract with 100 honors.

They score 180 points below the line for the six tricks at spades.

Above the line they score 100 for honors, 750 for the vulnerable small slam, and 500 for the rubber. It's a good thing for us that we managed to win a game during the rubber, since otherwise they would have received 700 points for winning the rubber!

WE	THEY
	500
	750
210	100
500	250
30	60
60	70
40	
	60
	120
	180

We now add up all the scores on both sides of the line. They have a total of 2090 points, and our total is 840 points. The difference is 1250 points, the amount by which they beat us.

If we keep the same partners for the next rubber, it is customary to carry the exact score of 1250 points forward. If we change partners, however, we write the score down to the nearest hundred. In this case we would treat 1250 points as though it were 1300 points (50 points or more counts as the next higher hundred, and 40 points or less as the next lower hundred), and we simply write down plus 13 for each of the opponents, and minus 13 for each of us.

Just as we avoided gloating when we were ahead, we must now lose with a good grace. Nobody expects us to stand up and cheer when we lose, but nobody will enjoy playing with us if we seem annoyed or heartbroken when we lose. It isn't easy to be a modest winner or a calm loser, but both of those attitudes are well worth cultivating.

REASONS FOR BIDDING

During the bidding your object is to get to a reasonable contract. This may or may not be a contract you can fulfill.

Sometimes you and your partner will hold poor cards, and sometimes good cards. Your side should gain points with good cards and should lose points with poor cards.

You can win points with your good cards either by making some contract of your own or by penalizing the opponents for their overbidding. Contrariwise, you can lose points with poor cards either by allowing the opponents to make some contract, or by overbidding and suffering a penalty.

There is nothing wrong or unsporting about deliberate overbidding. Your only question is: "Which way do I lose less?"

It is unsporting, of course, to overbid deliberately merely because you want to play the hand yourself. A player who does this sort of thing regularly is called a "bridge hog." It is desirable and sporting, however, to make a "profitable" sacrifice bid.

For example, suppose both sides are vulnerable. The side that wins the next game will score the rubber bonus of 500 points. If the opponents bid four hearts, you will lose 620 points by allowing them to make that contract. You are much better off if you bid four spades even if that can be set one trick. The opponents can collect 200 points by doubling your bid. This is not a profit, but it's far better to lose 200 points than 620.

Another point to remember about sacrifice bids is that sometimes the opponents can be pushed up one trick too high! Perhaps the opponents will not double you at four spades, but will go on to five hearts and be defeated. Now you really do make a profit on a hand which should have produced a loss for your side.

It will be obvious that you must have some idea of how many tricks you and your partner can make. You will need this not only for the situations in which both sides are bidding, but also when the opponents are silent.

2. Point Count Valuation

The easiest way to judge how many tricks your side can make is to value your hand according to the 4-3-2-1 point count. With a few key figures in your mind, you can bid as accurately as most of the world's leading bridge players.

THE POINT-COUNT TABLE

Cards	Value	Short Suits	Value
Each ace	= 4 points		
Each king	= 3 points	Each void suit	= 3 points
Each queen	= 2 points	Each singleton	= 2 points
Each jack	= 1 point	Each doubleton	= 1 point

(A "void" suit is a holding of no cards in a suit. A "singleton" is a holding of only one card in a suit. A "doubleton" is a holding of only two cards in a suit.)

Counting only the high cards, the total strength of the deck is 40 points. If everybody got an equal share of the strength, each player would have 10 points, or an "average hand."

Your side can usually make a game contract if you have a total of 26 points between you. Your side can usually make a small slam if the total point count is 33 points. Your side can usually make a grand slam (all thirteen tricks) if your combined count is 37 points.

If your side has only 20 to 25 points, you must usually be satisfied with a "part" score or less-than-game contract. If your side has fewer than 20 points, the opponents must have more than 20 and then it is probable that they can make some contract and that you cannot.

3. Opening Bids

You should think about making an opening bid whenever you have more than your share of the strength. As we have seen, an average hand counts 10 points, so that you begin to think about an opening bid whenever you have more than 10 points.

With 11 points, usually pass. Bid only when you have two five-card suits and when at least one of them is a major suit.

With 12 or 13 points, open the bidding whenever you have a fairly strong suit of five or more cards, or when you have two "biddable" four-card suits.

With 14 points, or more, *always* open the bidding. Never dream of passing with so strong a hand.

BIDDABLE SUITS

Your purpose in bidding a suit is to suggest it as the trump suit. Since the most important thing about the trump suit is its length, you should never suggest a trump suit unless you have some reason to suppose that your side will have more cards in that suit than the opponents hold.

For this reason, you never seriously* bid a suit in which you have only three cards. (And of course it would be even worse to bid a suit in which you hold fewer than three cards.)

If you have only three cards in a suit, some other player at the table is bound to have at least four cards in that suit. It is

---

* *Experts sometimes bid a short suit for some good reason. A beginner is much better off if he bids only his long suits.*

obviously foolish to bid a suit when you know in advance that somebody else is sure to have more trumps than you.

It is safe to bid a suit in which you hold only four cards, provided that the suit is headed by at least 3 points in high-card strength.

For example, the following are biddable suits:

Q J 7 5	A J 8 3
K 8 5 2	A K 9 5
A 7 4 3	A K Q J

The following four-card suits are not biddable:

Q 10 7 5	J 10 9 8	5 4 3 2

Any five-card suit is biddable. Any suit of more than five cards is likewise biddable.

REBIDDABLE SUITS

When you suggest a trump suit, your object is to find a suit in which your side holds eight or more cards. In a pinch, you may sometimes be satisfied with a combined holding of seven cards provided that those seven cards include most of the high trumps.

The more trumps you hold in your own hand, the fewer you need from your partner. When you have a strong five-card suit or any suit of six cards or more, you can afford to show this by bidding the suit and then rebidding it at a later turn. A suit that can safely be bid and rebid is called a "rebiddable suit."

A five-card suit is rebiddable if it is headed by any two of the four top cards. For example, the following suits are all rebiddable:

A K 8 5 3	K Q 8 5 3
A Q 7 6 4	K J 7 4 3
A J 6 5 2	Q J 6 5 4

Any suit of six or more cards is rebiddable.

CHOOSING THE OPENING BID

When you have enough strength for an opening bid, your best choice is almost always a bid of one in a suit. This will be true with hands that range from 12 points up to about 25 points in strength.

Assuming that you have the strength for a bid, begin with a bid of "one" in your longest suit. If you have two biddable suits *of equal length,* bid the *higher* ranking suit.

We will eventually discuss opening bids of more than one in a suit and opening bids of one or more notrump. At the beginning, however, it will do you no harm to open all biddable hands with a bid of one in a suit.

QUIZ ON OPENING BIDS

Assume that you are the dealer (and therefore first to speak) with each of the following hands. What do you say with each hand?

1. ♠ Q 8 2   ♥ K 9 7   ♦ K J 6 3   ♣ J 5 4

Pass. The count is only 10 points, and this is not enough for an opening bid.

2. ♠ K Q J 8 7 3 2   ♥ 9 8 4   ♦ 6 5   ♣ 3

Pass. The spades are very tempting, but the hand counts to only 9 points (6 points for the high spades, 1 point for the doubleton, and 2 points for the singleton).

3. ♠ A K 7 4   ♥ A 9 8   ♦ 10 5 3   ♣ J 6 2

Pass. The count is only 12 points, and you have neither a strong five-card suit nor two biddable four-card suits.

4. ♠ K Q J 8 7 3 2   ♥ A 8 4   ♦ 6 5   ♣ 3

Bid one spade. The count is 13 points (exactly one ace stronger than hand number 2), and you have a long, strong suit.

5. ♠ A K Q ♥ J 8 7 3 2 ♦ A 5 4 ♣ 9 6

Bid one heart. The count is 15 points, so you must make a bid of some kind. The spades are not biddable despite their strength. The long hearts are biddable. Remember that the most important feature of a trump suit is its length.

6. ♠ A K ♥ 7 6 5 4 3 2 ♦ A K Q J ♣ 4

Bid one heart. The diamonds are also biddable, but the longer suit should be bid first. The count is 20 points: 17 for the high cards, 1 for the doubleton, and 2 for the singleton.

7. ♠ 9 6 ♥ A K Q 3 ♦ A K J 5 4 ♣ 8 2

Bid one diamond. Hearts and diamonds are both biddable, but the rule is to show the longer suit first. The count is 19 points: 17 in high cards, and 1 for each of the doubletons.

8. ♠ 9 6 ♥ A K Q 3 ♦ A K J 5 ♣ 8 3 2

Bid one heart. Both red suits are biddable, and both are of equal length. The rule is to show the higher suit first. The count is 18 points: 17 in high cards, and 1 for the doubleton.

9. ♠ Q J 7 5 ♥ A 10 9 3 ♦ K Q J 5 ♣ 4

Bid one spade. This time you have three biddable suits, all of equal length. Bid the highest suit first. The count is 15 points: 13 in high cards, and 2 for the singleton.

10. ♠ A J 7 5 ♥ A K 9 3 ♦ A Q J 5 ♣ 4

Bid one spade. Again you have three biddable suits and choose the highest suit for your first bid. The hand is much stronger, but the opening bid is the same. The count is 21 points: 19 in high cards, and 2 for the singleton.

4. Responding
To Opening Bids

When both members of a partnership bid, one is called the "opening" bidder or the "original" bidder, and the other partner is called the "responder." Any bid made by the responder is called a "response."

Why should the opening bidder's partner respond? This question is easily answered if the responder has a strong hand: he will then want to bid towards a game or a slam.

The responder should likewise be willing to take some sort of action even with a fairly weak hand. Even at the low levels of bidding there are sound and unsound contracts, and the responder should do his share in steering the partnership toward a sound contract.

Before we discuss responses in detail, let's discuss a few general bidding habits. When you have played bridge often, your experience will show you that it is usually easy to win one trick more at a good trump suit than at notrump.

This fact has a great influence on bidding habits. When there is a choice between notrump and a trump contract you prefer a "major suit" (spades or hearts) over notrump, but you prefer notrump over a "minor suit" (diamonds or clubs).

The reason for these preferences is found in the scoring table. Bidding and making any of these will give you a game:

(a) three notrump
(b) four spades or four hearts (the major suits)
(c) five diamonds or five clubs (the minor suits)

You need one trick more for a game at a major suit than at notrump. Since that one additional trick is usually easy to find, you choose a major suit in preference to notrump when you have that sort of choice.

You need *two* tricks more for a game at a minor suit than at notrump. Since two additional tricks are usually hard to find, you choose notrump in preference to a minor suit when you have that sort of choice.

You don't always have a choice. Some hands will surely produce more tricks at a trump contract than at notrump. With such hands even a lowly minor suit should be chosen rather than notrump.

How can you recognize such hands? Usually by the short suits. A hand that contains a singleton or a void suit will usually play better at a trump suit than at notrump. A hand that contains *two* short suits practically begs you to name a trump suit.

Keep those facts in mind when you plan your responses— and in all later bids as well. Think of bidding a suit when you have a singleton or a void suit. Think of bidding notrump when you have no short suit. When you have a choice between a suit and notrump, favor a major suit but not a minor suit.

In your first response you may:

"Raise" your partner's suit (that is, bid for more tricks in the suit already named by your partner).

Bid a suit of your own.

Bid notrump.

Pass.

This choice will depend partly on your strength and partly on how many cards you have in each of the various suits. Let's consider your strength first.

RESPONDER'S POINT COUNT

When your partner opens the bidding he will usually have at least 13 points. Count up your own points and see how strong the combined hands are — remembering, of course, that your partner may have more than just a bare 13 points.

WHEN YOU HAVE 6 TO 10 POINTS: The combined count is at least 19 to 23 points. Your plan is to respond once, thus giving your partner the chance to take strong action if he has far more than a bare 13 points. If partner doesn't act strongly, you will pass any reasonable contract.

WHEN YOU HAVE 11 TO 12 POINTS: The combined count is at least 24 or 25 points. This is so close to the 26 points required for game that you will not only make a first response but will also speak up a second time to encourage your partner. If he has his bare 13 points, he will stop below game; but if he has slightly more than 13 points, he will accept your encouragement and go on to a game contract of some kind.

WHEN YOU HAVE 13 TO 16 POINTS: You know that the combined count is at least 26 points. You make sure of reaching some good game contract.

WHEN YOU HAVE 17 POINTS OR MORE: You take game for granted and concentrate on finding out whether or not to bid a slam.

Naturally, you don't keep your intentions a secret. You try to show your strength and the nature of your hand by the kind of response you make. An exchange of information takes place between you and your partner, and each of you should find out in good time whether to bid for a part score, a game, or a slam —and also which trump suits, if any, may be useful for the purpose.

All of this information is exchanged by the kind of bid you make—*not by the way in which you make the bid!* A beginner sometimes sounds tremulous when he has a poor hand, or confident when he has a good hand. An experienced player makes all of his bids in the same tone of voice.

When you become a really good player, you will discover that it is very bad form to vary the tone of voice in bidding. Every game has its code and its traditions, and when you get past the beginning stage you must respect the code.

RAISING PARTNER'S SUIT

Consider a *raise of partner's suit* when you have "trump support" that consists of:

(a) Four or more cards in that suit, or
(b) Three cards headed by queen or better

For example, you may raise with Q-3-2 of partner's suit, or with any four cards. Do not raise, however, when you have only two cards in his suit even if those two cards happen to be the ace and king.

If these rules are followed, you and your partner will seldom bid high in a suit without eight or more trumps between you. At worst, he will occasionally bid a suit such as K-7-5-3, and you may raise with Q-6-2. This is not a very strong trump suit, but it is good enough for a low contract.

Raise your partner's suit from one to two if you have trump support and a count of 6 to 10 points for the hand as a whole.

Do not raise your partner's suit immediately if you have a count of 11 or 12 points, even if you have good trump support. Bid some side suit, and raise your partner's suit later. This delayed raise shows your hand accurately: trump support with a count of 11 or 12 points.

Raise your partner's suit from one to three (a "jump raise") if you have *strong* trump support (four or more trumps) and 13 to 16 points for the hand as a whole.

Raise your partner's suit from one to four (a "shutout" bid) if you have five or more trumps, a singleton or void suit, and no more than 9 points in high cards. This bid is intended to reach game and to shut the opponents out of the bidding at the same time.

RESPONDING WITH A NEW SUIT

Bid one of a new *biddable* suit with a count of 6 to 16 points in the hand as a whole. This is possible only if your suit is higher than your partner's suit.

When your partner's suit is higher than your suit, you cannot bid just one of your suit. You must raise the level of the bidding by going to two of your suit. This is safe only when you have at least 9 points. Hence a response of two in a lower suit than the opening bid shows a hand of 9 to 16 points.

What should you do with fewer than 6 points? Pass. Just let your partner struggle with his opening bid of one.

What should you do with 6 to 8 points when you have no higher suit to bid? Look for trump support, since you may be able to raise partner's suit. If you have no raise, make a "convenience response" of one notrump.

What should you do with more than 16 points? Look for a way to explore slam possibilities. The best method is to bid one more than necessary (a "jump bid") in a new suit.

RESPONDING IN NOTRUMP

A response of one notrump shows a hand with 6 to 9 points that contains no biddable suit higher than your partner's suit and that isn't good enough for a raise of partner's suit. With fewer than 6 points you would pass; and with more than 9 points you would find some other response.

This *response of one notrump shows a weak hand* and is merely a convenience response. Most other notrump bids show a very definite type of hand.

Bid two notrump (a jump response) with 13 to 15 points,

no singleton or void suit, and at least 3 points in each of the unbid suits. This indicates a strong hand with something in every suit.

Bid three notrump (a jump response) with 16 or 17 points, no singleton or void suit, and at least 3 points in each of the unbid suits. This bid shows so much strength that your partner may easily be able to consider a slam.

CHOOSING THE RESPONSE

If your partner opens the bidding with a minor suit, show a new suit if you can. If your partner opens with a major suit, consider a raise.

If you are considering a jump bid in notrump, prefer notrump to a minor suit. When your choice is between notrump and a major suit, prefer the major suit.

If you have two suits of your own, respond in the longer suit. If both are of equal length, respond in the higher suit. (This is the same principle that is followed by the opening bidder.)

5. Rebids By The Opening Bidder

When partner raises your suit, count up your hand again, and *add 1 point for each trump over four* that you hold. In other words, add 1 point if you hold a five-card trump suit; 2 points for a six-card suit; and so on.

AFTER A SINGLE RAISE

Assume that your partner has 7 or 8 points for his raise, and add those points to your own new count of points.

This new total will tell you whether to stop short, try for a game, or simply bid a game:

When the combined strength is about 22 points or less, pass.

When the combined strength is about 24 points, make an attempt to reach game.

When the combined strength is 26 points or more, make *sure* of reaching game.

South	West	North	East
1♥	Pass	2♥	Pass
? *			

---

* The question mark indicates that it is South's turn to speak. You are South and you are asked to supply the correct action. You have already bid one heart; and you are now about to speak again. In each of the examples throughout the book the question mark means, "What do you say here?"

What should you do in each of the following cases if you hold:

11.　♠ A 3 2　♥ A K 8 7 5　♦ Q 7 4　♣ 6 3

Pass. Your count was 14 points to begin with—13 points in high cards, and 1 point for the doubleton. You may now add 1 point for the fifth heart, bringing your count up to 15 points.

Add these to your partner's count of 7 or 8 points, and the total is only 22 or 23 points. There is no chance for game with so low a total, so you pass.

12.　♠ A 3 2　♥ A K 8 7 5 2　♦ Q 7 4　♣ 6

Bid three hearts. Your count was 15 points to begin with—13 points in high cards, and 2 points for the singleton. You may now add 2 points for the fifth and sixth trump, bringing your total up to 17 points.

Add these to your partner's count of 7 or 8 points, and the total is 24 or 25 points. There is a chance for game, since partner may have 9 points instead of only 7 or 8. Hence you "invite" the game by bidding three hearts.

Partner will pass with 7 points; will bid game with 9 points; and will toss a mental coin with 8 points.

13.　♠ A 3 2　♥ A K 8 7 5　♦ Q 7 4　♣ K 3

Bid two notrump. Your count was 17 points to begin with —16 points in high cards, and 1 point for the doubleton. You may now add 1 point for the fifth heart, bringing your count up to 18 points.

Add these to your partner's total of 7 or 8 points, and the total is 25 or 26 points. There is an excellent chance for game, and you bid an "invitational" two notrump. Partner may pass with 7 points; but he will tend to bid three hearts with 8 points and good hearts, and he will bid either four hearts or three notrump with 9 points.

14. ♠ A 3 2 ♥ A K 8 7 5 2 ♦ A 7 4 ♣ 6

Bid four hearts. Your count was 17 points to begin with—
15 points in high cards, and 2 points for the singleton. You may
now add 2 points for the fifth and sixth hearts, bringing your
total up to 19 points.

Add these to your partner's total of 7 or 8 points, and the
total is 26 or 27 points. Since there is no doubt about the 26
points, you must bid game without further ado. Never make the
mistake of merely "inviting" a game when you *know* you have
the material for a game bid.

AFTER A DOUBLE RAISE

Your partner's jump raise is "forcing" to game. As we will
see later on, certain bids create a partnership understanding that
the two partners will not drop the bidding until game has been
reached. Such a bid is called a forcing bid.

In this case, your partner's double raise shows 13 to 16
points. This strength, added to whatever you have for your
opening bid, brings the partnership total up to the 26 points
usually needed for game. Whenever it is clear that the combined
hands contain 26 points or more, a game contract should be
reached.

After your partner's double raise, you should go on to game
either in your own suit or in notrump. The choice depends on
the nature of your hand.

If you have no singleton and no void suit, with your strength
well distributed, try for game in notrump. Contrariwise, prefer
to bid game in the suit if you have a singleton or a void suit, if
your strength is concentrated in one or two suits, or if your
trump suit is more than five cards long.

South	West	North	East
1 ♥	Pass	3 ♥	Pass
?			

What should you do if you hold:

15.   ♠ A 3 2   ♥ A K 8 7 5   ♦ Q 7 4   ♣ 6 3

Bid four hearts. Your revised point count of 15 plus partner's 13 to 16 points total 28 to 31 points. You know you must go on to game, and you bid the game in hearts because of the weak doubleton in clubs.

16.   ♠ A 3 2   ♥ K Q 8 7 5   ♦ Q 7 4   ♣ K 3

Bid three notrump. Your strength is well distributed, and your distribution is balanced (no singleton or void suit, and only one doubleton), so you can suggest game in notrump rather than the heart suit.

North will pass three notrump if he likewise has balanced distribution. Otherwise he will return to hearts.

17.   ♠ A 3 2   ♥ K Q 8 7   ♦ Q 7 4   ♣ K J 3

Bid three notrump. This is especially desirable when you have bid a four-card suit. If North insists on hearts, however, you will take his word for it.

18.   ♠ A 3 2   ♥ K Q 8 7 5   ♦ K Q 4 3   ♣ 3

Bid four hearts. Since you have a singleton, you do not consider a final contract in notrump. Just proceed to game in the suit.

AFTER A RESPONSE OF ONE NOTRUMP

Your partner's bid announces that he has a poor hand, counting only 6 to 9 points. The combined hands will not contain the 26 points needed for game unless you have at least 17 points in your own hand.

If you have fewer than 17 points, you must avoid getting too high. Let your partner play the hand at one notrump whenever your own hand is reasonably balanced. (A balanced hand is one that contains no singleton or void suit and not more than one doubleton.) Make a minimum rebid in your original suit or in some new suit if your distribution is very unbalanced.

South	West	North	East
1 ♥	Pass	1 NT	Pass
?			

19.　♠ A 6 5　♥ A K 8 7 5　♦ Q 7 4　♣ J 3

Pass. You have a count of 15 points—14 in high cards, and 1 point for the doubleton.

Add these to the 6 to 9 points shown by your partner's response, and it becomes clear that the combined count is between 21 and 24 points. No game is possible, so your only concern is to avoid getting too high.

It would be a mistake to bid two hearts even though you have a "rebiddable" five-card suit. You are not compelled to rebid a rebiddable suit.

20.　♠ A 6 5 3　♥ A K 8 7 5　♦ Q 7 4　♣ 3

Bid two hearts. Your count is still only 15 points, so you do not expect to reach a game contract. You rebid because your distribution is unbalanced (you have a singleton), so that the hand will probably play better at two hearts than at one notrump.

21.　♠ K 6 5　♥ A K 8 7 5　♦ K J 7 4　♣ 3

Bid two diamonds. You still do not expect to reach game, since your count is only 16 points (14 points in high cards, and 2 points for the singleton).

You rebid because you have unbalanced distribution. The hand will play better at one of the red suits than at notrump. If North has more diamonds than hearts he will prefer diamonds and pass; if he has more hearts than diamonds, however, he will take you back to two hearts. Notice that this does not raise the contract.

When you have 17 points or more, you can afford to hope for a game contract. Do not pass your partner's bid of one notrump. Raise in notrump if you have balanced distribution, or make further bids in some suit if you have unbalanced distribution.

South	West	North	East
1♥	Pass	1 NT	Pass
?			

22. ♠ A 6 5   ♥ A Q J 7 5   ♦ A 7 4   ♣ J 3

Bid two hearts. You have a count of 17 points—16 points in high cards, and 1 point for the doubleton. You can afford to proceed even though North has only 6 to 9 points, but you must proceed with caution.

A contract of two hearts should be safe even if North has only 6 or 7 points. You may hear more from North if he happens to hold his maximum of 9 points.

23. ♠ A 6   ♥ A K 8 7 5   ♦ K J 7 4   ♣ J 3

Bid two diamonds. You have a count of 18 points—16 points in high cards, and 2 points for the two doubletons. You can afford to make a second bid in the hope that North will show some enthusiasm even though he cannot hold more than 9 points.

24. ♠ A 6   ♥ A K 8 7 5   ♦ K J 7   ♣ Q J 3

Bid two notrump. You have a count of 19 points—18 in high cards, and 1 point for the doubleton. The combined count is at least 25 points, and it may well be more.

North will go on to three notrump if he has 8 or 9 points, but will pass if he has only 6 or 7 points.

25. ♠ A 6   ♥ A K 8 7 5   ♦ K Q 7   ♣ K J 3

Bid three notrump. You have a count of 21 points—20 in high cards, and 1 point for the doubleton. The combined count will be 27 points even if North has the bare minimum for his response of one notrump.

Do not make the mistake of "inviting" a game when you can go right ahead and bid it.

26.　♠ A 6　♥ A K J 7 5　♦ K Q 7 5 2　♣ 3

Bid three diamonds. You have a count of 20 points—17 in high cards, 2 for the singleton, and 1 for the doubleton.

Add these to the 6 to 9 points shown by North's response, and you see that the combined count is 26 to 29 points—ample for game. Hence you make a jump bid. This bid is "forcing," and you are sure of reaching a game contract of some sort.

27.　♠ A 6　♥ A K Q J 7 5　♦ K 7 5　♣ 6 3

Bid three hearts. You have a count of 19 points—17 in high cards, and 2 for the doubletons. Moreover, you may count 1 point each for your fifth and sixth hearts even though North hasn't raised the suit. Your own heart holding is so extremely powerful that you may treat the suit as though it had been raised.

AFTER A RESPONSE OF TWO NOTRUMP

Your partner's response is a jump bid and is therefore forcing to game. His response showed exactly 13 to 15 points, so that you can add your own points and get a very accurate idea of the combined strength.

In general, raise to game in notrump when you have balanced distribution. Bid your original suit or some new biddable suit when you have unbalanced distribution.

South	West	North	East
1♥	Pass	2 NT	Pass
?			

28.　♠ K 3　♥ A Q J 7 4　♦ Q 9 3　♣ K 7 5

Bid three notrump. You have balanced distribution and strength in each suit. It should be at least as easy to make three notrump as four hearts.

29.　♠ 8 3　♥ A Q J 7 4　♦ K Q 3　♣ K 7 5

Bid three hearts. Your worthless doubleton in spades is a weak point, so you should steer away from notrump.

30. ♠ 8 ♥ A Q J 7 4 ♦ K Q 3 ♣ K 7 5 2

Bid three hearts. Your distribution is unbalanced, and you should therefore rebid in a suit rather than in notrump.

31. ♠ 8 ♥ A Q J 7 4 ♦ K Q 3 2 ♣ K 7 5

Bid three diamonds. You have a second biddable suit, and should show it to hint that notrump is unsatisfactory.

AFTER A RESPONSE IN A NEW SUIT

When your partner bids his own suit he asks for a chance to bid a second time, but doesn't promise to use that chance! He will bid a second time if he has fair strength, but he will pass at his second turn if he has a weak hand.

Before we discuss your rebid, let's first note what we know about the responding hand. Your partner's response may be in a suit that is *higher* than yours or it may be in a *lower* suit.

He can bid a higher suit with a bid of only one. Such a bid of one in a suit is sometimes called a "one-over-one" response.

Your partner cannot bid his suit at the level of one if it is lower than yours. Instead, he must bid *two* of his suit. Such a response is called a "two-over-one" response. (A bid of two in a higher suit—for example two spades in response to one heart— is called a "jump" response and is not considered a "two-over-one" response.)

A one-over-one response shows a count of 6 to 16 points. A two-over-one response shows a count of 9 to 16 points.

This difference will often affect the way you rebid. Let's first consider how you rebid when your partner has made a one-over-one response.

It is up to you to make some rebid that will describe your hand and that will thus put your partner in a good position to judge how far the combined hands will stretch.

If you have opened the bidding with 12 to 16 points, you

will make a *minimum* rebid of some kind; if you have 17 to 19 points, you will make a *strong* rebid; with more than 19 points you will make a *forcing* rebid.

You can make a *minimum* rebid (showing 12 to 16 points) by bidding one notrump, two of your original suit, or two of your partner's suit. You may even show a new suit. The choice depends on the nature of your hand.

South	West	North	East
1 ♥	Pass	1 ♠	Pass
?			

32. ♠ 7 5   ♥ A Q J 9   ♦ K 8 4 3   ♣ A 8 2

Bid one notrump. You have a count of 15 points—14 in high cards and 1 for the doubleton. You must therefore make a minimum rebid.

You cannot rebid the four-card heart suit, you have no new suit to show, and you cannot raise spades because you lack trump support for that suit. Hence the only bid left to you is one notrump.

33. ♠ 7 5   ♥ A Q J 9 4   ♦ K 8 4   ♣ A 8 2

Bid two hearts. The count is the same as the previous example, but this time the heart suit is rebiddable.

34. ♠ 7 5 3 2   ♥ A Q J 9   ♦ K 3   ♣ A 8 2

Bid two spades. The count is still the same, but this time you have trump support for your partner's suit.

35. ♠ 7 5   ♥ A Q J 9 4   ♦ A J 4 3 2   ♣ 2

Bid two diamonds. You have a count of 15 points—12 in high cards, 2 for the singleton, and 1 for the doubleton. You must make a minimum rebid, but in this case you can show your other suit. This hints that your distribution is unbalanced.

If your hand totals 17 to 19 points you should make a *strong* rebid. Bid two notrump, jump to three of your own suit, or jump to three of your partner's suit. Here again, the choice depends on the nature of your hand.

36. ♠ 7 5 ♥ A Q J 9 ♦ K Q 4 3 ♣ A Q 2

Bid two notrump. You have a count of 19 points—18 in high cards, and one point for the doubleton. This jump bid indicates your strength and is forcing to game for all practical purposes. The bid also indicates that you have balanced distribution (no singleton or void suit) and strength in each of the unbid suits.

37. ♠ 7 5 ♥ A K J 9 4 2 ♦ A 9 4 ♣ A 8

Bid three hearts. You have a count of 18 points—16 points in high cards, and 2 points for the doubletons. You can be very nearly certain that the combined hands contain 26 points or more, in which case there should be a good play for game in hearts or in notrump. Depending on the nature of his hand, North will either raise hearts, rebid his spades, or try for game in notrump.

38. ♠ 7 5 3 2 ♥ A Q J 9 ♦ K 3 ♣ A K 2

Bid three spades. You have a count of 18 points—17 in high cards, and 1 point for the doubleton. Since you have four-card trump support for your partner, your strong rebid takes the form of a raise. Depending on the nature of his hand, North should proceed on to four spades, show support for your hearts, or try for game at three notrump.

39. ♠ Q 5 ♥ A Q J 9 4 ♦ A Q J 3 2 ♣ 2

Bid three diamonds. You have a count of 19 points—16 in high cards, 2 points for the singleton, and 1 point for the doubleton. You may be nearly certain that the combined hands contain at least 26 points and that there will be a reasonable play for game. If your partner has no support for either of the red suits, he may have a very long spade suit and then your spades will be sufficient support.

With 20 points or more you can make a *very strong* rebid. Jump to three notrump, raise your partner's suit to game, or make a jump bid in an entirely new suit. Once again, the choice depends on the exact nature of your hand.

40.　♠ Q 5　♥ A Q J 9　♦ A Q 8 4　♣ A Q 5

Bid three notrump. You have a count of 22 points—21 points in high cards, and 1 point for the doubleton. No matter how "light" North's response may have been, you are willing to play this hand in a game contract. The combined count should be easily more than 26 points. Three notrump is a game contract, and if North makes any further bid, you are entitled to assume that he is interested in a slam.

41.　♠ 8 5　♥ A K Q J 9 6 2　♦ A Q 5　♣ 2

Bid four hearts. You have a count of 22 points, although this may not be obvious at first glance. You have, of course, counted 16 points in high cards, 2 points for the singleton, and 1 point for the doubleton. Thus far, the count is only 19 points. Your heart suit is so powerful, however, that you are entitled to treat it as though it had been raised by your partner. You may therefore count three extra points for the fifth, sixth, and seventh hearts. This brings your count up to 22 points.

42.　♠ K J 8 5　♥ A Q J 9　♦ A K 6 3　♣ 2

Bid four spades. This strong bid shows a count of 20 points or more. In this case you have exactly 20 points—18 in high cards and 2 points for the singleton. This energetic jump raise guarantees at least four-card trump support, including some high trumps.

43. ♠ K J 5 ♥ A Q J 9 4 ♦ A K Q 3 ♣ 2

Bid three diamonds. This jump bid is forcing to game, and may be made on a hand of almost unlimited strength. In this case you have a count of 22 points—20 points in high cards, and 2 points for the singleton. You may be quite confident that there will be a very good play for game in one of the red suits, in spades, or perhaps in notrump.

North must help you find the best game contract by showing the nature of his hand. If he has a rebiddable spade suit, he must tell you so in order that you may be able to raise the spades. Otherwise, he may be able to show support for one of the red suits. If he has strength in the only unbid suit (clubs) he may indicate this fact by bidding three notrump.

AFTER A TWO-OVER-ONE RESPONSE

Your partner's response in a new suit asks you to give him another chance to bid. In this case, your partner's response shows a minimum of 9 points. You can therefore expect a game contract when you have about 17 points, and you can hope for a game contract even if you have slightly less than 17 points.

With unbalanced distribution, make a rebid in your first suit, in some new suit, or by means of a raise in partner's suit. With balanced distribution and strength in the two unbid suits, rebid in notrump.

South	West	North	East
1 ♥	Pass	2 ♣	Pass
?			

44. ♠ A 5 2 ♥ A Q J 9 ♦ K 8 6 4 ♣ 3 2

Bid two notrump. You have a count of 15 points—14 in high cards, and 1 point for the doubleton. In this case you use notrump as a rebid of convenience. You cannot rebid the four-card heart suit, you have no new suit to show, and you cannot raise your partner's clubs. The only remaining possibility is to make your rebid in notrump.

45. ♠ A 5 2 ♥ A Q J 9 4 ♦ K 8 6 ♣ 3 2

Bid two hearts. You have a count of 15 points—14 in high cards, and 1 for the doubleton. Since your heart suit is rebiddable, you simply make a minimum rebid in that suit.

46. ♠ 7 5 2 ♥ A Q J 9 ♦ A J 9 5 ♣ Q 2

Bid two diamonds. You have a count of 15 points—14 in high cards, and 1 for the doubleton. Your hearts are not rebiddable, and you cannot raise the clubs. Since your diamonds are biddable, you show the nature of your hand by a minimum rebid in diamonds.

47. ♠ 7 ♥ A Q J 9 4 ♦ A J 9 5 2 ♣ 8 2

Bid two diamonds. You have a count of 15 points—12 in high cards, 2 for the singleton, and 1 for the doubleton. Your natural course is to make your rebid in your other biddable suit. Note that your partner cannot tell, when you bid two diamonds, whether you have two four-card suits or two five-card suits. This will become clearer to him as the bidding proceeds.

48. ♠ 7 5 ♥ A Q J 9 ♦ A Q J 5 ♣ Q J 2

Bid three clubs. You have a count of 18 points—17 in high cards, and 1 point for the doubleton. With 17 points or more you are willing to get to the level of three (calling for nine tricks).

49. ♠ A 5 2 ♥ A Q J 9 4 2 ♦ K 8 ♣ Q 2

Bid three hearts. You have a count of 18 points—16 in high cards, and 2 for the doubletons. The heart suit is so strong, moreover, that you should count either 1 or 2 points for the fifth and sixth hearts. Your jump bid indicates that you think the combined hands contain at least 26 points. The fact that you have made your jump bid in hearts indicates that you have a very powerful heart suit which needs practically no support from your partner.

50. ♠ A J 9   ♥ A Q J 9   ♦ K Q 6 4   ♣ Q 2

Bid three notrump. You have a count of 20 points—19 in high cards, and 1 for the doubleton. No matter how "light" your partner's response may have been, the combined hands should give you a very easy play for game. Note that your bid also indicates balanced distribution and strength in both of the unbid suits.

51. ♠ Q 5   ♥ A K J 9 5   ♦ A Q J 4   ♣ K 3

Bid three diamonds. You have a count of 22 points—20 in high cards, and 2 for the doubletons. Your jump bid indicates that the combined hands contain at least 26 points. The nature of your rebid indicates that you have a second biddable suit. For all North can tell you may be prepared to raise clubs later on. Then again, you may have two more powerful suits of your own. His not to reason why. He simply bids his own hand, realizing that your bid is forcing until game is reached.

52. ♠ 4   ♥ A K J 9 5   ♦ J 4   ♣ A J 6 3 2

Bid four clubs. This jump indicates unusually good distribution. This means that you have at least ten cards in hearts and clubs combined, with correspondingly short suits elsewhere. You would not try so hard for game in a minor suit (clubs) if you thought that a game at notrump were possible.

In this case you have a count of only 17 points—14 in high cards, 2 for the singleton, and 1 for the doubleton. Nevertheless, your support for your partner's suit is so very good that you may hope for game.

53. ♠ 4   ♥ A K J 5   ♦ K Q J 4   ♣ A J 6 3

Bid three diamonds. Note the difference between this and hand No. 51. You have a count of 21 points—19 in high cards, and 2 for the singleton. You know that the combined hands contain more than 26 points, so that the play for game should be very easy.

Your best course is to make a jump bid in diamonds rather than raise directly to four clubs or five clubs. You will raise the clubs at your next turn, and will thus bid three suits at your first three turns to bid. A player who bids three suits indicates that he is very short in the fourth suit, so that your partner will realize that you are short in spades. This may be very important for the proper bidding of his hand.

54. ♠ 4 ♥ A K Q J 7 3 2 ♦ A Q 5 ♣ Q 2

Bid four hearts. This bid indicates an independent heart suit (one that needs no support from partner) and a count of about 20 points. In this case you have a count of 24 points—18 in high cards, 2 for the singleton, 1 for the doubleton and 3 for the fifth, sixth, and seventh hearts.

THE MEANING OF A JUMP BID

Any bid of more than necessary is a jump bid. A bid of exactly one more than necessary means that the partnership can safely bid up to game.

The bidding has been:

North	East	South	West
1 ♥	Pass	?	

a. Which bids are non-jump?

The non-jump bids in response to one heart are: one spade, one notrump, two clubs, two diamonds, and two hearts. Each of these is the lowest bid that can legally be made.

b. Which bids are a jump of one more than necessary?

The single jump bids in response to one heart are: two spades, two notrump, three clubs, three diamonds, and three hearts. Each of these bids is forcing until game is reached.

c. Which bids are multiple jumps?

The multiple jump bids in response to one heart are: three or more in spades or notrump; four or more, in clubs or diamonds. Jump bids in notrump always show strong hands, but the multiple jump bids in suits are used partly to shut the opponents out of the bidding and partly to reach a satisfactory contract.

Note that a multiple jump bid *in a suit* is weaker, not stronger, than a single jump bid! Don't make the mistake of thinking that the more you jump the more strength you show.

Whenever you can tell from the count of your own hand and from the bids made by your partner that the combined count is easily 26 points, you should make a single jump bid of some kind. This jump bid will tell your partner not to pass until game has been reached. You can then bid comfortably without worrying that your partner will pass prematurely.

6. Rebids By The Responder

Your partner has made an opening bid.

You have already responded.

Your partner has rebid.

Now it is up to you again.

Should you seek safety in a pass or in the cheapest possible bid? Or should you make a strong bid of some kind? The answers to these questions depend on the nature of your partner's bidding and the nature of your own hand. If both are weak, you naturally seek safety. If both are strong, you naturally bid boldly. If one is weak and the other is strong, you must use your judgment.

Using your judgment is not really as vague as it sounds. It depends partly on experience, which you will gain as you play, and partly on simple arithmetic.

Experience will teach you, if you have a good memory! You may find, for example, that you and your partner are defeated in more than half of your game contracts. No good player expects to make every game he bids, but he does count on fulfilling about two games for every one that he loses. Your conclusion must therefore be that you and your partner are overbidding.

When you come to this sort of conclusion, do not go to the other extreme of crawling into your shell and bidding timidly. Just assume that you and your partner need 27 or 28 points for game instead of the usual 26 points. That will give you a proper margin of safety. Eventually your play of the cards will improve, and you will be able to go back to the normal requirement.

Arithmetic is your surest guide. You have already made a first response, promising strength within definite limits. If your strength is near the bottom limit, you must thereafter proceed cautiously; if it is near the top limit, you may show a further sign of life.

For example, suppose your first response promised 6 to 9 points. You will tend to refuse any invitational bids with 6 or 7 points, but you will accept an invitation if you have 8 or 9 points.

We are now ready to discuss your rebids as a responder in greater detail.

WITH 6 TO 9 POINTS

Your first response has very nearly told your whole story. Unless your partner's rebid shows a very strong hand, you should look for your first convenient chance to get out of the bidding. When your partner has made a minimum rebid, your best course as a general rule is to pass. If partner has bid two suits, show as cheaply as possible which suit you prefer. If you don't like either suit, pass and hope for the best rather than make matters worse by rebidding your own suit.

North	East	South	West
1 ♥	Pass	1 ♠	Pass
1 NT	Pass	?	

55.　♠ K J 7 5 3　♥ 5 2　♦ Q 8 4　♣ 9 6 5

Pass. You have a count of 7 points—6 in high cards and 1 for the doubleton. Your partner's rebid of one notrump shows that he has no more than 16 points. Hence the combined total cannot be more than 23 points, and game must be out of the question. One notrump is a reasonable contract, and your safest course is therefore to pass.

56. ♠ K J 10 9 7 5 3 ♥ 5 2 ♦ 4 ♣ 9 6 5

Bid two spades. Once more you have a count of 7 points—
4 for the high cards, two for the singleton, and 1 for the doubleton. As in the previous example, you do not expect to reach and
make a game contract.

Since one notrump is not a safe contract, however, you rebid
your very long spade suit. In general, a hand will play better at
a suit than at notrump when one of the partners has a very long
suit and correspondingly short suits elsewhere.

North	East	South	West
1 ♥	Pass	1 ♠	Pass
2 ♥	Pass	?	

57. ♠ K J 7 5 3 ♥ 5 2 ♦ Q 8 4 ♣ 9 6 5

Pass. Your partner's bid still shows the same maximum of
16 points, and game is still out of the question. You are reasonably
satisfied with the contract of two hearts, and should pass to avoid
getting too high.

58. ♠ K J 10 9 7 5 3 ♥ 5 2 ♦ 4 ♣ 9 6 5

Bid two spades. The hand will surely play well in spades
because you have so many of them, and your partner may have
only a five-card heart suit. It would not be a bad mistake to let
your partner play the hand at two hearts. If you had three small
hearts instead of only two, a pass would be the correct procedure.

North	East	South	West
1 ♥	Pass	1 ♠	Pass
2 ♠	Pass	?	

59. ♠ K J 7 5 3 ♥ 5 2 ♦ Q 8 4 ♣ 9 6 5

Pass. Since your partner has raised your suit, you are entitled to count the fifth spade as one extra point. Your count is
therefore 8 points, but the combined total is only 24 points at
most. Game is out of the question, and you should therefore pass.

60. ♠ K J 10 9 7 5 3 ♥ 5 2 ♦ 4 ♣ 9 6 5

Bid three spades. You are now entitled to count one point each for the fifth, sixth, and seventh spades. Your total count is therefore 10 points, and there is a chance that the combined count is 26 points. You bid three spades to "invite" a game.

North will go on to four spades if he has his maximum of 16 points or perhaps with 15 points. If he has only 13 or 14 points, he will pass at three spades.

North	East	South	West
1 ♥	Pass	1 ♠	Pass
2 ♦	Pass	?	

61. ♠ K J 7 5 3 ♥ 5 2 ♦ Q 8 4 ♣ 9 6 5

Pass. The situation is still the same. Your partner has no more than 16 points, and your own count is still only 7 points. You are reasonably satisfied with a diamond contract, and therefore pass.

62. ♠ K J 7 5 3 ♥ Q 8 4 ♦ 5 2 ♣ 9 6 5

Bid two hearts. As before, you do not expect to reach game. In this case you prefer hearts to diamonds and therefore show this fact as cheaply as possible. This bid is not considered a raise but is merely a preference.

63. ♠ K J 10 9 7 5 3 ♥ 5 2 ♦ 4 ♣ 9 6 5

Bid two spades. You are not satisfied with either hearts or diamonds, and you therefore rebid your very long suit.

WITH 10 TO 12 POINTS

Even if your partner has a minimum opening bid, the combined count will be very close to the 26 points usually needed for a game. You can well afford to make a second response even if your partner has shown no extra strength in his rebid.

If you can discover a fit in a major suit or in notrump, it

may be possible to make a game contract even with only 25 points. You will not, however, insist on a game contract.

You will make your second response to let your partner know that you have a moderately strong hand (10 to 12 points) and the decision is then up to him. He will know about your hand, but you will not know about his. It is therefore clearly up to him to decide whether or not the combined total is enough for game.

The nature of your second bid depends upon the nature of your hand. You may be able to support some suit that your partner has bid. If not, you may wish to rebid your own suit, or even to bid an entirely new suit. If none of these courses seems desirable, your hand should then be suitable for a bid in notrump.

North	East	South	West
1 ♥	Pass	1 ♠	Pass
2 ♦	Pass	?	

64. ♠ K J 7 5 3   ♥ Q 9 4 3   ♦ K 3   ♣ 6 5

Bid three hearts. You have a count of 11 points—9 in high cards and 2 for the doubletons. You are therefore entitled to make a second strength-showing bid.

As we have just seen, a bid of only two hearts would not show strength but would be merely a preference. You must therefore go to *three* hearts in order to show some sign of life.

65. ♠ K J 7 5 3   ♥ K 3   ♦ Q 9 4 3   ♣ 6 5

Bid three diamonds. This is the same as hand No. 64, with the red suits exchanged. You show your strength by raising the suit you prefer.

66. ♠ K J 7 5 3   ♥ K 3   ♦ 6 5   ♣ Q J 4 3

Bid two notrump. You have a count of 12 points—10 in high cards and 2 for the doubletons. You must make a second strength-showing bid, but cannot support either of the red suits and do not wish to rebid the somewhat moth-eaten spade suit. Since you have strength in the only unbid suit, you may indicate this fact by making a rebid in notrump.

WITH MORE THAN 12 POINTS

Since you have 13 points or more in your own hand, and since you know that your partner has at least 13 points for his opening bid, you know that the combined total is at least 26 points. If you have not already made a jump bid of some kind, you should do so at this moment. If you have already made a jump bid, however, it is not necessary to do so again.

North	East	South	West
1 ♥	Pass	1 ♠	Pass
2 ♦	Pass	?	

67.　♠ A J 7 5 3　♥ Q 9 4 3　♦ A 3　♣ 6 5

Bid four hearts. You have a count of 13 points—11 in high cards, and 2 for the doubletons. You have excellent four-card support for hearts, and therefore know that a sound heart suit is available.

Nothing more is needed for a game; you know that the combined hands contain at least 26 points, and you know that a sound trump suit has been found. In such a situation, you should avoid guesswork or misunderstanding. Bid the game at once.

68.　♠ A Q J 7 5 3　♥ 4 3　♦ Q 6　♣ A 6 5

Bid three spades. You have a count of 15 points—13 in high cards, and 2 for the doubletons. Since no jump bid has been made up to this moment, you should make one now. The bulk of your strength is in your long, powerful spade suit, and you should therefore make your jump bid in spades.

69. ♠ K J 7 5 3 ♥ K 3 ♦ Q 6 ♣ A Q 3 2

Bid three notrump. You have a count of 17 points—15 in high cards, and 2 for the doubletons. Since no jump bid has been made up to this moment, you must make one now to notify your partner that the combined hands are good for a game. Your strength is well distributed and your distribution is balanced, so your jump rebid is made in notrump.

RAISING A REBID SUIT

When your partner rebids a suit in spite of the fact that you have not raised him, he shows that he has at least one card more than would be needed for a biddable suit. Hence you can afford to raise him with one trump less than the usual requirements for raising.

In other words, you can raise a rebid suit with any three cards or with two cards headed by a queen, king or ace.

If your partner bids a suit *three* times without support, he shows a suit that is about two cards longer than an ordinary biddable suit. Hence you can afford to raise such a strong suit with any two cards or with a singleton high card.

PRACTICAL ADVICE FOR PRACTICE

You now know enough about bidding to play some bridge, but you need a lesson on the play of the cards before you can get the most out of a practice game. Turn to Chapter 12 and read on to the end of the book. Then you will be ready for some actual play, and you can return to Chapters 7 to 11 at your leisure.

7. Slam Bidding

There will usually be a reasonable play for a small slam contract when you and your partner hold a combined count of at least 33 points. Until you have become an experienced player, however, you should avoid reaching a slam with a bare minimum of 33 points unless you and your partner have established a good fit in a sound trump suit, together with a reasonably strong side suit.

There will usually be a reasonable play for a grand slam when you and your partner hold a combined count of 37 points or more. Until you become a very experienced player, however, you should make it a rule not to bid grand slams. (Break this rule when your hand is so strong that the temptation to bid a grand slam is overpowering. And even then you will often have only regrets to show for the experience!)

There are three general methods of bidding a slam:

DIRECT SLAM BIDDING—used when one member of the partnership has a very strong hand and can make the slam decision without help.

SLAM EXPLORATION—used when neither partner is strong enough to decide without help.

THE BLACKWOOD CONVENTION—used when one player can decide for or against a slam upon finding out how many aces his partner holds.

Before taking up these three methods in detail, absorb these words of warning: Your first step in considering slam possibilities is to check the combined count. If your most optimistic addition does not total 33 points, be satisfied with a game contract. There is no glory in bidding a slam that you cannot make.

DIRECT SLAM BIDDING

Sometimes it is easy to tell from the early bidding that a slam can probably be made. If you are very sure that a slam can be made, do not keep it a secret. Your partner may not be able to read the situation as clearly as you can.

One way of getting to the slam is simply to *bid it!* This is the correct procedure whether you are the opening bidder or the responder.

South	West	North	East
1 ♥	Pass	3 ♥	Pass
?			

70. ♠ A 5   ♥ A Q J 9 4   ♦ A 3 2   ♣ K Q 9

Bid six hearts. You have a count of 22 points—20 in high cards, 1 for the doubleton, and 1 point for the fifth heart. (Remember that you may count a point for each trump over four when your suit has been raised by your partner.)

Your partner's jump to three hearts shows 13 to 16 points. His minimum of 13 points added to your 22 points gives a partnership total of at least 35 points. Since only 33 points are needed for the slam, the combined total of 35 points should give you a very comfortable slam contract.

71. ♠ A K   ♥ A K J 9 4   ♦ A K 2   ♣ K 10 9

Bid seven hearts. You have a count of 27 points—25 in high cards, 1 point for the doubleton, and 1 point for the fifth heart.

Your partner's raise to three hearts shows 13 to 16 points, so that you are sure of a combined total of at least 40 points. This accounts for practically every high card in the deck. The opponents will be lucky if they hold as much as a queen.

North	East	South	West
1 ♥	Pass	1 ♠	Pass
3 ♥	Pass	?	

72. ♠ A Q J 7 5   ♥ K 8 4   ♦ A 3 2   ♣ K 3

Bid six hearts. You have a count of 18 points—17 for high cards and 1 for the doubleton. Your partner's jump rebid shows a very powerful heart suit and a count of 17 to 19 points.

As you can see, the combined count is at least 35 points, and you are sure of a powerful trump suit (hearts) and a strong side suit (spades).

SLAM EXPLORATION

You will not always be absolutely sure that a slam can be made. When you are willing to explore the possibilities, you should make an "invitational" bid.

If your partner's bidding then gives you further encouragement, you proceed on to the slam; and if he makes discouraging bids, you stop at a game contract. Sometimes it is necessary to get slightly beyond game in order to invite the slam. This type of slam invitation should be avoided if possible, since there is no advantage in bidding past game unless you are strong enough to make a slam.

The bidding has been:

South	West	North	East
1 ♥	Pass	3 ♥	Pass
?			

73. ♠ 7 5   ♥ A J 10 9 4   ♦ A 3 2   ♣ A K 9

Bid four clubs. You have a count of 18 points—16 in high cards, 1 for the doubleton, and 1 for the fifth heart. Your partner's jump raise shows a count of 13 to 16 points. The combined total is therefore 31 to 34 points.

Since 33 points are needed for a slam, you cannot be sure that this hand is worth a slam. You extend an invitation by bidding four clubs. Note that it would not be necessary to bid the clubs if you were merely trying to reach a game in hearts. You could simply bid four hearts instead of four clubs and let it go at that. Your only logical reason for bidding a new suit at the ten-trick level is to hint at a slam and to ask for partner's cooperation.

Note that you don't really have a biddable club suit since you hold only three clubs. This is allowable when you are exploring slam possibilities provided that you and your partner have "agreed" upon a trump suit. In this case, you have agreed upon hearts, and any other suit is considered only a slam try.

If North responds to your slam try with a bid of four hearts, he will be notifying you that his hand doesn't permit him to encourage your slam ambition. If North bids four spades (*showing the ace of that suit*) he will automatically force you to bid at least five hearts, thus indicating that his hand is worth bidding past game. Likewise North may make some other bid that is higher than four hearts, and any such bid would encourage you to go on to a slam.

74.   ♠ 7   ♥ A Q 10 9 4   ♦ A 3   ♣ K Q J 7 5

Bid four clubs. You have a count of 20 points—16 points in high cards, 2 points for the singleton, 1 point for the doubleton, and 1 point for the fifth heart. Note that this time you have a real club suit, whereas in the previous example you merely had top cards in clubs without length in the suit. Your partner cannot tell which type of hand you hold, but he does know that you are making a slam try.

If North gives you the slightest encouragement, you will proceed to slam with this hand. If he "signs off" by returning to four hearts over your slam try of four clubs, you may make a further slam try by bidding four notrump or five hearts. (A bid of four notrump in this situation would have a special meaning, as you will see very soon in the explanation of the Blackwood Convention.)

75. ♠ 7   ♥ A Q 10 9 4   ♦ 8 3   ♣ K Q J 7 5

Bid four hearts. You have a count of only 16 points—12 in high cards, 2 for the singleton, 1 for the doubleton, and 1 for the fifth heart.

Since your partner's double raise shows only 16 points at most, the combined hands contain a maximum of 32 points. At best, therefore, you will be short of the 33 points needed for a slam. You must also consider the possibility that your partner does not have the absolute maximum of 16 points, in which case you will be even farther short of the 33 points needed for a slam.

THE BLACKWOOD CONVENTION

In some situations you are sure of a very powerful trump suit and a very good side suit. Such hands will often produce twelve tricks if you can be sure that the opponents are not in a position to cash two tricks before you can get started.

To guard against this danger, you must make sure that you and your partner hold three aces between you. There may still be some danger that your opponents can take two immediate tricks in the fourth suit, but you may have some way of knowing that this danger does not exist. (For example, you may have the king, or a singleton, in the fourth suit. The opponents can therefore take only one trick in it.)

The Blackwood Convention is a method of finding out how many aces are contained in your partner's hand. After a suit has been *bid by one partner and raised by the other partner,* a bid of four notrump has this special meaning: "Partner, tell me by your next bid *how many aces you hold.*"

The partner's response will not indicate any length or strength in the suit that he happens to bid. His response shows only *the number of aces in his hand.* The method is as follows:

NUMBER OF ACES	RESPONSE TO 4 NT
None	5 ♣
One	5 ♦
Two	5 ♥
Three	5 ♠

The Blackwood Convention will not help you make an impossible slam, in the play of the cards. It is only a bidding weapon, and like any weapon it must be used carefully lest it turn against you.

South	West	North	East
1 ♥	Pass	3 ♥	Pass
?			

76. ♠ K 3   ♥ A K J 9 4   ♦ K Q J 7 3   ♣ 2

Bid four notrump. You have a count of 21 points—17 in high cards, 2 for the singleton, 1 for the doubleton, and 1 for the fifth heart. (Remember that you count 1 point extra for each trump over four when your partner has raised your trump suit.) Your partner's jump raise shows that he has 13 to 16 points. The combined hands therefore contain at least 34 points and perhaps as many as 37.

You expect to make a slam very comfortably if the opponents are unable to take the first two tricks. They might do so if they hold two aces, and this is barely possible.

You use the Blackwood Convention to find out how many aces your partner holds. If he holds only one ace, you will be satisfied with a contract of five hearts. If he holds more than one ace, you will confidently bid a slam in hearts.

77. ♠ A 3   ♥ A Q J 9 4   ♦ K Q J 7   ♣ K 5

Bid four notrump. You have a count of 23 points—20 in high cards, 2 points for the doubletons, and 1 point for the fifth heart.

You know that your partner has 13 to 16 points, so that the

combined count is 36 to 39 points. There is no doubt in your mind about a small slam, provided your partner has at least one ace.

78.　♠ 9 3　♥ A Q J 9 4　♦ K Q J 7　♣ 8 5

Bid four hearts. You have a count of only 16 points.

Even if your partner has a maximum of 16 points, the combined total will be only 32 points. This is less than the slam requirement, even when you have made your most optimistic addition.

RESPONDING TO A 4 NT BLACKWOOD BID

South	West	North	East
1 ♥	Pass	3 ♥	Pass
4 NT	Pass	?	

79.　♠ Q J 4　♥ Q 10 8 2　♦ 10 8　♣ A K Q 3

Bid five diamonds. You have one ace and must show that fact by making the standard response.

It doesn't matter how good or how bad the rest of your hand may be. Your partner has asked you to tell him how many aces you hold, and you must give him exactly this information, nothing more and nothing less.

80.　♠ Q J 4　♥ Q 10 8 2　♦ A 8　♣ A J 4 3

Bid five hearts. This response shows that you have exactly two aces. In responding to a Blackwood Convention bid of four notrump, you ask no questions but merely give the requested information.

81.　♠ A 4 2　♥ Q 10 8 2　♦ A 8　♣ A 7 4 3

Bid five spades. This response shows three aces. Note that your partner must now bid at least six hearts. This need not be feared, since he surely has the type of hand in which a slam depends on finding aces in your hand rather than kings and queens. He can hardly expect to find more than three aces in your hand, so his slam contract must be quite safe.

THE 5 NT BLACKWOOD BID

The biggest thrill in bridge is to bid and make a grand slam. By means of the Blackwood bid of five notrump you may explore grand slam possibilities, but do not consider a grand slam unless you are quite sure that the combined hands contain a very strong trump suit and a good side suit.

The player who has bid a Blackwood four notrump can see the number of aces in his own hand and can tell from his partner's response how many aces his partner holds.

When you discover that all four aces are present in the combined hands, you may then realize that a grand slam is possible, provided your partner holds the right number of kings.

Having already bid *four notrump,* you now bid *five notrump.* This is another bid with a special meaning: "Partner, show me how many kings you hold!"

As in the case of the response to four notrump, your partner shows the number of kings he holds by an "artificial" bid:

NUMBER OF KINGS	RESPONSE
None	6 ♣
One	6 ♦
Two	6 ♥
Three	6 ♠
Four	6 NT

When you know the number of kings in your partner's hand you can add your own kings to find the combined total. In general, don't bid a grand slam when a king is missing. Most important of all, ask for kings only when the combined hands include all four aces, a very strong trump suit, and a good side suit.

South	West	North	East
1 ♥	Pass	3 ♥	Pass
4 NT	Pass	5 ♥	Pass
?			

82. ♠ A 3   ♥ A Q J 9 4   ♦ K Q J 7   ♣ K 5

Bid five notrump. You have a count of 23 points. Your partner's response of five hearts showed two aces and you are now interested in a grand slam.

Grand slams often depend on aces and kings as well as combined points. You have already discovered that your partner has both of the missing aces. If he also has both of the missing kings, you will bid seven hearts. If he responds with six clubs, indicating no kings, or six diamonds, showing one king, you will bid six hearts and that will end your bidding.

83. ♠ A 3   ♥ A Q J 9 4   ♦ K Q J   ♣ 9 5 3

Bid six hearts. You have a count of 19 points—17 in high cards, 1 for the doubleton, and 1 for the fifth heart.

Since your partner's maximum is only 16 points, the combined count cannot be more than 35 points. As we know, 37 points are usually needed for a grand slam, so this hope must be abandoned. You may have your hands full making a small slam since the combined count may conceivably be as low as 32 points.

84. ♠ K 3   ♥ A Q J 9 4   ♦ K Q J   ♣ K Q 3

Bid six hearts. Your partnership lacks one ace.

GENERAL ADVICE ON SLAM BIDDING

When you are an absolute beginner, you will probably be very timid about bidding slams and even about trying for them. After you have played bridge for a few months, you will very often go to the other extreme by bidding slams far too recklessly. When you are an experienced player, you will hit a balanced stride.

Do not expect to fulfill every slam that you bid. Bad luck will sometimes defeat a slam that was justifiably bid. But you should expect to fulfill about two or three slams to every one that is defeated. If you lose more than that number, tighten up a trifle in your slam bidding.

8. Notrump Bidding

For an opening bid in notrump you should have a very definite type of hand. Your hand must have:

(a) "shape"
(b) "size"
(c) "stoppers"

SHAPE: A hand with long suits and short suits will almost always play better at some suit than at notrump. For play at notrump you prefer the type of hand that has no very long suit and no very short suit.

The "shape" of a hand is determined by the length of the suits in that hand. The "flattest" shape consists of four cards in one suit and three cards in each of the other suits (4-3-3-3 distribution, in bridge language). The most "freakish" shape consists of all thirteen cards in the same suit (13-0-0-0).

The shapes that are best for notrump are:

     4-3-3-3   4-4-3-2   5-3-3-2

Avoid bidding notrump when the shape of your hand is anything but one of these three.

SIZE: When you bid notrump your bid will indicate your "size," or strength, almost to the exact number of points.

An opening bid of 1 NT shows 16 to 18 points.

An opening bid of 2 NT shows 22 to 24 points.

An opening bid of 3 NT shows 25 to 27 points.

(*Count only high cards—not short suits—for notrump.*)

What should you do when you have the right shape, the right stoppers, but the awkward size of 19 to 21 points? Such hands are too strong for an opening bid of one notrump, but not strong enough for an opening bid of two notrump.

The solution to the problem is to open such a hand with one of a suit. At your next turn, make a jump rebid in notrump.

If you break these rules you may still reach the correct contract, but more by luck than by good management. It is also possible to cross a busy street with your eyes closed and live to tell the story!

STOPPERS: A "stopper" is a card or group of cards in a suit that will win a trick when that suit is led. When you play a hand at notrump, your opponents will try to win tricks in some long suit. If you cannot stop them from doing so, they will defeat your contract.

When you open the bidding with one or more notrump, you should have a stopper in each suit. In a pinch, you may bid one notrump (but not two or three) with one suit unstopped, but even in this case you should have either three or more cards in the suit or no doubleton worse than K-x.*

The ace is a sure stopper, because you can surely take a trick with the ace when that suit is led.

The king and queen of a suit (K-Q) make a sure stopper together. The opponents may capture the king with their ace, but then your queen will win a trick.

The guarded king (K-x or K-x-x)* is a sure stopper if the suit is led by the player at your left. You play last to such a trick, and you will win the trick with your king if nobody plays the ace. If the ace is played, you follow suit with one of your small cards and your king will be good for the next trick in that suit.

Similar reasoning will show you that the ace and king of

---

* In bridge writing each "x" indicates a small card, below honor rank.

the same suit (A-K) are a double stopper. So are K-Q-J or A-Q-J.

Other single stoppers are K-J-10 and Q-J-10. Among the *almost* sure stoppers are K-J-x and Q-J-x. Even K-10-x or Q-10-x are fairly respectable stoppers.

QUIZ ON OPENING BIDS IN NOTRUMP

What do you bid, as dealer, with each of the following hands:

85.　♠ K J 4　♥ A Q 7 2　♦ Q J 6　♣ K 9 8

Bid one notrump. You have a count of 16 points, with a stopper of some sort in each suit and proper notrump shape. Never open the bidding with one of a suit when you have a perfect opening bid of one notrump.

86.　♠ A 10 5　♥ A Q 7 2　♦ K Q 8 3　♣ K 7

Bid one notrump. You have a count of 18 points, the maximum allowed for this opening bid. Do not be disturbed by the fact that you have two four-card suits. This hand will probably play at least as well at notrump as at a suit.

87.　♠ K 5　♥ Q J 7　♦ K J 8 3 2　♣ A Q 8

Bid one notrump. You have a count of 16 points, with a stopper of some sort in each suit. Do not be steered away from notrump by the fact that you have a five-card suit. The 5-3-3-2 shape is all right for notrump provided that your doubleton is headed by at least the king.

88.　♠ K J 4　♥ Q J 7 2　♦ A J 6　♣ K 9 8

Bid one heart. The shape is perfect, and you have a stopper of some sort in each suit, but your count is only 15 points. This is not enough for an opening bid of one notrump, and it does not pay to "lie" about these things.

89. ♠ K J 4 ♥ Q J 7 2 ♦ A J 6 ♣ A K 8

Bid one heart. You have notrump shape and a stopper of some sort in each suit, but your count is 19 points. This is too much for an opening bid of one notrump. Bid your suit to begin with, and make a jump bid in notrump at your next opportunity.

90. ♠ K 4 ♥ Q J 8 7 2 ♦ A Q 6 3 ♣ A 8

Bid one heart. You have a count of 16 points and a stopper of some sort in each suit, but the shape is wrong for notrump. Avoid an opening bid of one notrump when you have two doubletons, and never even consider such an opening bid when you have a singleton or a void suit.

91. ♠ A Q 5 ♥ K J 7 3 ♦ A Q 6 3 ♣ 9 8

Bid one heart. You have a count of 16 points, and proper notrump shape, but you have a weak doubleton in clubs. Do not make an opening bid of one notrump when you have a doubleton headed by anything lower than the king.

92. ♠ K Q 8 ♥ A J 9 5 ♦ K Q J ♣ A Q 5

Bid two notrump. You have proper notrump shape, every suit well stopped, and a count of 22 points. However, do not be overcome by the magnificence of your hand when your turn comes to make further bids. Remember that your opening bid has told your full story.

93. ♠ A Q 9 ♥ K Q 10 ♦ A Q ♣ K Q J 9 4

Bid two notrump. You have proper notrump shape, stoppers in every suit, and a count of 23 points. It would be a mistake to bid the clubs first when the opening bid of two notrump tells your whole story in one bid.

94. ♠ A Q 9 ♥ A Q 10 ♦ J 8 ♣ A K Q 9 4

Bid one club. You have proper notrump shape and a count of 22 points, but you lack a stopper in diamonds. You should not make an opening notrump bid of any description with so weak a holding in any suit. Open the bidding with one club and make a game bid or a forcing bid at your next turn. If your partner responds in diamonds, you can jump to three notrump. If he bids any other suit, you can jump raise his suit or make a jump rebid in clubs.

95.　♠ A Q 9　♥ A Q 10　♦ A K J　♣ A Q 8 3

Bid three notrump. You have a count of 26 points with notrump shape and every suit well stopped.

RESPONDING TO ONE NOTRUMP

When your partner opens the bidding with one notrump, he shows 16 to 18 points. Your hand will produce a game with 10 points, and perhaps with as little as 8.

Always remember that 26 points are usually enough for game. The more points your partner shows by his bids, the less you have to contribute to make a game.

WITH BALANCED DISTRIBUTION: If you have fewer than 8 points, game is either remote or impossible. For example, you may have 7 points, and your partner may have his maximum of 18 points, but the total is still only 25 points—1 point short of game.

These principles are the basis for your method of responding to one notrump when you have balanced distribution:

WHEN YOU HOLD	GENERAL RESPONSE
0 to 7 points	Pass
8 or 9 points	2 NT
10 to 15 points	3 NT or 3 of a suit
16 points or more	Bid towards a slam

WITH UNBALANCED DISTRIBUTION: When you have a singleton or void suit, the combined hands will probably play better at a suit than at notrump. Nevertheless, it does not pay to bid a suit when your hand is woefully weak.

With only 3 or 4 high-card points, pass one notrump. Your partner will probably be defeated, but nothing serious will happen to a low contract that has not been doubled. (If an opponent doubles, bid your long suit when your hand is that weak.)

With 6 or 7 points in high cards and unbalanced distribution, bid your long suit. Your partner may bid again, but even so it will be better to play the hand at three of your long suit than at one notrump.

With 5 or 6 points, you have a choice of action. It is usually wise to pass. Bid your suit if it is unusually long or if you have two very short suits.

QUIZ ON RESPONDING TO ONE NOTRUMP

North	East	South	West
1 NT	Pass	?	

What is your response with each of the following hands?

96. ♠ 8 5 3 ♥ 9 7 6 ♦ 8 6 4 ♣ 7 5 3 2

Pass. This is an absolutely hopeless hand, and no action of any kind can even be considered. Your partner will surely be defeated at one notrump, but this cannot be helped.

97. ♠ J 5 3 ♥ Q 7 6 ♦ K 6 4 ♣ J 5 3 2

Pass. This hand is far from hopeless since your count is 7 points, but it is just under the requirement for a raise.

98. ♠ Q 5 3 ♥ Q J 7 ♦ K 6 4 ♣ J 5 3 2

Bid two notrump. You have a count of 9 points, and can therefore raise to two notrump. The combined count is between 25 and 27 points.

99. ♠ 8 5 3 ♥ 9 7 6 ♦ K 4 ♣ A Q 9 7 4

Bid two notrump. Once again your count is 9 points, with your length in clubs as an added asset. Your partner has some strength in clubs as part of his opening bid, and the club suit will be very useful in the play of the hand at notrump. Do not bid two clubs, which shows a poor hand, when you can encourage your partner with a raise to two notrump.

100.　♠ 8 5 3　♥ Q 7 6　♦ K 4　♣ A Q J 7 4

Bid three notrump. You have a count of 12 points, which is more than enough for a raise to game. Do not make the mistake of merely encouraging your partner when you are strong enough to bid game at once.

101.　♠ A Q J 7 4　♥ Q 7 6　♦ K 4　♣ 8 5 3

Bid three spades. This is the same as hand No. 100, except that the black suits have been exchanged. You are perfectly willing to let your partner play the hand at three notrump, but you can suggest a game at spades in the meantime. If partner has good support in spades, he will raise to four spades; otherwise he will bid three notrump.

It is often easier to make ten tricks at a good major suit than nine tricks at notrump, and that is why you have made a jump bid in spades. It is seldom easier to make eleven tricks in a minor suit than nine tricks at notrump, and that is why you did not mention clubs in hand No. 100.

102.　♠ A Q J 7　♥ Q 7 6　♦ K 4 2　♣ 8 5 3

Bid three notrump. You have a count of 12 points, which is more than enough for this raise to game. You do not bother to bid the spades in this case since the suit is only four cards in length.

103.　♠ A Q J 7 4　♥ K 7 6　♦ A 4 2　♣ K 8

Bid three spades. You have a count of 17 points in high cards, and therefore know that the combined count is at least 33 points even if your partner has the weakest possible opening bid of one notrump. You intend to bid a slam eventually, but you do not know whether to bid it in spades or in notrump.

Note that your partner cannot tell whether you are trying for a game or for a slam when you jump to three spades. With hand No. 101, for example, you bid three spades and stopped at a game contract. With this hand, you jump to three spades with the intention of reaching a slam sooner or later.

104.　♠ A Q J 7　♥ K Q 7 2　♦ A Q　♣ K J 9

Bid seven notrump. You have a count of 22 points, and therefore know that the combined count is 38 to 40 points. The opponents may hold a queen or a jack, but cannot hold any other high card. It should therefore be very easy for your partner to take all thirteen tricks.

105.　♠ J 8 7 5 3　♥ 6　♦ Q 7 3 2　♣ 8 5 3

Pass. You have a count of 3 points in high cards, and may count two points for the singleton if you play the hand at spades. Your distribution is unbalanced, but your suit is neither long nor particularly strong. You cannot be sure that you will be better off at spades than your partner will be at one notrump.

106.　♠ J 8 7 5 3 2　♥ 6　♦ Q 7 3 2　♣ 5 3

Bid two spades. This is almost the same hand as No. 105, but the spade suit is now six cards in length. Despite the miserable weakness of the hand, you may feel sure that you will win more tricks at spades than your partner would win at notrump.

107.　♠ A Q 8 7 5　♥ 6 3　♦ 9 5 4　♣ 8 5 3

Bid two spades. This is not a rescue, since your partner might be perfectly happy at one notrump. If your partner shows a strong hand by rebidding, you may even take a chance and proceed on to game. It would not be a serious mistake to pass this hand, but it is quite sound to bid two spades.

RESPONDING TO TWO NOTRUMP

When your partner opens with two notrump, he shows 22 to 24 points. You need very little to bring the combined total to 26 points. Hence, in general:

(a) Respond with 4 points or more.
(b) Pass with 3 points or less.
(c) Bid for slam with 11 points or more.

CHOICE OF RESPONSE: Raise to three notrump with balanced distribution. Bid a long suit, if you have one, especially when you have unbalanced distribution. The fundamental principle is always the same—prefer a long suit when you can, and fall back on notrump when you have no long suit.

BIDDING A WEAK HAND: In rare cases you may respond to two notrump even though you have fewer than the normal 4 points. This is proper only when you have a six-card or longer suit and a singleton or void suit on the side. Such a hand will play much better at your suit than at notrump, although there is a strong possibility that you will take a loss at either contract.

SLAM BIDDING: With 33 points in the combined hands, there is usually a fair play for a slam. If you are nervous about slams, increase this requirement to about 35 points but don't give up slam bidding altogether.

Thus, you may confidently bid a slam when you hold 11 points or more opposite an opening bid of two notrump. Your partner has 22 to 24 points, and the combined total is therefore 33 to 35 points.

QUIZ ON RESPONDING TO TWO NOTRUMP

North	East	South	West
2 NT	Pass	?	

What is your response with each of the following hands?

108. ♠ 7 5 2 ♥ 9 6 3 ♦ Q 7 5 4 ♣ J 8 2

Pass. You have only 3 points, and there is therefore no reason to bid. The chances are very strong that your partner will not be able to make a game.

109. ♠ 7 5 2   ♥ 9 6 3   ♦ Q 7 5 4   ♣ Q 8 2

Bid three notrump. This hand is only slightly stronger than hand No. 108, but the difference is enough to give you a chance for a game contract. With 4 points or more, you respond to your partner's opening bid of two notrump.

110. ♠ K 5 2   ♥ 9 6 3   ♦ K 7 5 4   ♣ K 8 2

Bid three notrump. This is, of course, a very good hand for this response. In hand No. 109 you held the minimum for a raise to three notrump, and in this case you hold just about the maximum. With any more, you would think about a slam.

111. ♠ K 9 6 5 2   ♥ 6 3   ♦ Q 7 5   ♣ 9 6 3

Bid three spades. If partner has a good fit for your major suit, you are willing to play the hand at four spades. If he goes to three notrump, you will be content to let him stay there.

112. ♠ K 9 6 5 3 2   ♥ 6   ♦ Q 7 5   ♣ 9 6 3

Bid three spades. If partner can raise to four spades, you will be content. If partner bids three notrump, you will go on to four spades anyway. This hand should play far better at spades than at notrump.

113. ♠ Q 7 5   ♥ 6 3   ♦ K 9 6 5 2   ♣ 9 6 3

Bid three notrump. This is the same hand as No. 111 except that the spade and diamond suits have been exchanged. You would be willing to consider a game in a major suit, but as between three notrump and five of a minor you prefer the easier game at notrump.

114. ♠ Q 7 5   ♥ 6   ♦ K 9 6 5 3 2   ♣ 9 6 3

Bid three diamonds. This is the same as hand No. 112 except that the spade and diamond suits have been exchanged. With a six-card suit and a singleton you are willing to insist on a diamond contract rather than play for game at three notrump.

If your partner bids three notrump, you will go on to four diamonds.

115. ♠ K 5 2   ♥ Q 6 3   ♦ K 7 5 4   ♣ K 8 2

Bid six notrump. You have a count of 11 points, and therefore know that the combined count is 33 to 35 points. This should give your partner a very sound play for his slam.

116. ♠ K Q 6 5 3   ♥ 6 3   ♦ K 7 5   ♣ K 8 2

Bid three spades. You intend to go on to a slam, but you are not sure whether the hand should be played at spades or notrump. If North's next bid is three notrump, you will raise to six notrump. If North's next bid is four spades, you will go on to six spades instead of six notrump.

117. ♠ K J 6 5   ♥ A 3   ♦ K 7 5   ♣ A Q 9 5

Bid seven notrump. You have a count of 17 points, and your partner's count is 22 to 24 points. Hence the combined count is at least 39 points. The opponents cannot possibly have more than 1 point—which means that they cannot have more than one jack in high cards. Your partner should be able to take thirteen tricks without the slightest difficulty.

RESPONDING TO THREE NOTRUMP

When your partner opens with three notrump, he shows 25 to 27 points. Any response by you is considered a slam try. You may confidently bid a slam when you have 8 points or more, since then the combined total will be 33 to 35 points.

REBIDDING AFTER NOTRUMP

When you have opened the bidding with one notrump, you have described your hand almost completely. The main job of further bidding is up to your partner. Your partner may give you certain choices, however, and you may therefore have to think about a rebid.

IF YOUR PARTNER BIDS TWO OF A SUIT: You must decide whether to pass or rebid. Your partner has a very weak hand (otherwise he would bid three of his suit or raise notrump) and you should pass about nine times out of ten. Bid two notrump or three of his suit if you have 18 points and good help for his suit; otherwise pass.

IF YOUR PARTNER BIDS TWO NOTRUMP: You must either bid three notrump or pass. Uusually, go on to game. Pass if you have only 16 points, with marked weakness in some suit; otherwise bid three notrump.

IF YOUR PARTNER BIDS THREE NOTRUMP: Pass. You are in a game contract, and that is where you should stay.

IF YOUR PARTNER BIDS THREE OF A SUIT: Keep going until game is reached. Raise a major suit with good support (especially four-card support); otherwise bid three notrump.

QUIZ ON REBIDDING AFTER NOTRUMP

South	West	North	East
1 NT	Pass	2 ♠	Pass
?			

118. ♠ K Q 4　♥ A J 7 2　♦ K 9 4　♣ K J 5

Pass. You have good support for spades, but only 17 points.

119. ♠ K Q 4　♥ A J 7 2　♦ A 9 4　♣ K J 5

Bid three spades. You have good support for spades and 18 points, so you are entitled to act again. It would be equally correct to bid two notrump instead of three spades.

120. ♠ A J 7 2　♥ K Q 4　♦ A 9 4　♣ K J 5

Bid three spades. Once again you have good support for your partner's suit and 18 points. In this case, since you have four-card support for spades, you would not even consider bidding two notrump rather than three spades.

121. ♠ Q 7 3 ♥ A J 7 2 ♦ A K 4 ♣ K J 5

Pass. You have 18 points, but the support for spades is only mediocre. Remember that you do not act again unless you have 18 points *plus* excellent support for your partner's suit.

South	West	North	East
1 NT	Pass	2 NT	Pass
?			

122. ♠ K 7 5 ♥ A J 7 2 ♦ K 9 4 ♣ K Q 5

Bid three notrump. You have only 16 points, but you have strength in each of the four suits. This is enough to encourage you to proceed to game.

123. ♠ 8 7 5 ♥ A Q J 7 ♦ K 9 4 ♣ A Q 5

Pass. You have only 16 points, and you have marked weakness in spades. With such a hand you are willing to settle for a part-score contract.

124. ♠ 8 7 5 ♥ A Q J 7 ♦ K J 4 ♣ A Q 5

Bid three notrump. You have one weak suit (spades) but 17 points. Since you have more than the minimum, you go on to game.

South	West	North	East
1 NT	Pass	3 ♥	Pass
?			

125. ♠ K 7 5 ♥ K 9 3 ♦ A J 8 5 ♣ K Q 6

Bid four hearts. You have fairly good support for hearts, so you can afford to raise your partner's suit. It would not be bad to bid three notrump rather than three hearts. The choice is a very close one.

126. ♠ A J 5 ♥ 9 8 3 ♦ A J 10 5 2 ♣ A Q

Bid three notrump. Since you do not have good support for hearts, you have no choice in this matter. You must keep bidding until game is reached, however, since your partner's jump bid is forcing to game.

9. Opening Two-Bids

When you are dealt an immensely powerful hand of unbalanced distribution, you have a special way of beginning the bidding. You open by bidding two in a suit. This is forcing until game is reached.

SHAPE: An opening bid of two in a suit should show unbalanced distribution: a void suit, a singleton, or at worst two doubletons.

STRONG SUIT: The hand must contain at least one strong suit, and perhaps two. A "strong" suit is a five-card or six-card suit headed by at least three honors; or any suit of more than six cards.

SIZE: Add up your point count as usual. You need at least 25 points for a bid of two in your suit.

You are dealer with each of the following hands. What is your opening bid?

127.　♠ A Q J 7 3　♥ A K 5　♦ A K 4　♣ K 8

Bid two notrump. You have a strong suit and the right size, but you do not have the right shape for an opening bid of two in a suit. With your balanced distribution you should make a strong opening bid in notrump. With even a jack more you would open with three notrump.

128.　♠ A Q J 7 3　♥ A K 5 4　♦ A K　♣ K 8

Bid two spades. This is the same hand as No. 127 except that the shape has been improved. You are now entitled to open the hand with two in your best suit.

129. ♠ A J 8 7 3   ♥ A K J 4   ♦ A K   ♣ K 8

Bid two notrump or one spade. There is no completely satisfactory opening bid for this hand. The spade suit is not strong enough for an opening two bid, and the shape of the hand is wrong for an opening bid of two notrump. An opening bid of only one spade is an underbid that may cause you to miss a game. In a situation of this kind you must choose the least of evils. It is hard to predict whether one spade or two notrump will produce the most satisfactory results with the hand.

130. ♠ A J 8 7 3   ♥ A K J 9 4   ♦ A K   ♣ A

Bid two spades. Only one of your long suits is strong enough for an opening two bid, but that is enough. Note that you make your opening bid in the higher suit even though this is weaker than the hearts. The general rule is followed: with suits of equal length, bid the higher suit first.

131. ♠ A K Q 7 3   ♥ A K Q 7 3   ♦ 3 2   ♣ 2

Bid one spade. You have two excellent suits and the right shape for an opening bid of two, but the hand does not measure up to the right size. If your partner cannot respond to an opening bid of one, you are not likely to miss a game.

RESPONDING TO A TWO-BID

When your partner opens with a bid of two in a suit you are not supposed to pass until game is reached. It doesn't matter how weak your hand may be. If you respect your partner's judgment, you will be a good partner and will help him reach his game.

Your response is based partly on your strength and partly on your distribution (just like any bid). If you have a weak hand, announce it as soon as possible by making a "weakness response." If you have fair strength, speak up boldly; there may be a play for slam.

THE WEAKNESS RESPONSE: Bid two notrump in response to your partner's opening two-bid if you hold fewer than 6 points *in high cards*. Don't add points for short suits.

Sometimes it will go against the grain to bid notrump when you have very long suits, but do not worry; you will have the chance to show your distribution later if your partner is at all interested in it. Your first response must show only one definite fact, and that is your high-card count.

POSITIVE RESPONSES: With 6 or more points *in high cards,* make a positive response. At this point, that means any bid other than two notrump. Your response should be a raise if you have good support for your partner's suit; a suit of your own if you have a strong suit to show; or *three* notrump if you have general strength without either support for partner's suit or a good suit of your own.

North	East	South	West
2 ♥	Pass	?	

132.　♠ J 9 7 3 2　♥ 6　♦ Q J 7 5 4 3　♣ 5

Bid two notrump. You have a count of only 4 points in high cards, and must therefore make a "weakness response." Your partner will bid again. Unless he jumps to game, you will be able to show your long suit (or suits).

133.　♠ J 9 7　♥ Q J 7 5　♦ 9 6 5 4 2　♣ 5

Bid two notrump. Once again you have only 4 points, and must therefore make a weakness response. At your next turn you will make sure to raise the hearts. This will indicate a hand with good heart support but without the high card strength needed for a positive response.

134.　♠ K 9 7　♥ Q J 7 5　♦ 9 6 5 4 2　♣ 5

Bid three hearts. This time you have a count of 6 points in high cards and can therefore afford to make your positive response immediately. Since you have excellent trump support, your positive response takes the form of a raise.

135. ♠ K Q J 7 5   ♥ 7 5   ♦ 9 6 5 4 2   ♣ 5

Bid two spades. You have a count of 6 points and are therefore entitled to make an immediate positive response. Since you have a strong suit of your own, your positive response takes the form of a bid in your suit.

136. ♠ K 9 7 2   ♥ 7 5   ♦ K J 5   ♣ Q 8 5 3

Bid three notrump. Since you have a count of more than 6 points, you are entitled to make a positive response. You cannot raise hearts, and you have no strong suit of your own, and you must therefore make your bid in notrump. A bid of only two notrump would be the weakness response, so you bid three notrump to show your strength.

REBIDDING AFTER A TWO-BID

BY THE OPENER: If your partner has responded with two notrump, you must usually give up any hope of bidding and making a slam. Proceed towards game in the usual way.

In other words, bid a new suit if you have one. Otherwise, rebid your original suit or, with 5-4-2-2 distribution, raise to three notrump.

If your partner has made a *positive response* to your opening bid of two, think of a slam. Your partner has at least 6 points, and you have at least 25 points. Slam is not far away. If a fit can be found in a strong suit, bid a slam; otherwise be satisfied with a game contract.

BY THE RESPONDER: Make sure of reaching a game no matter how weak your hand may be. If you have 10 points or more, make sure of reaching a slam. With 6 to 9 points, make your first positive response and continue with strong bidding if you fit your partner's trump suit; but continue with minimum bidding *to a game contract* even if you have no fit for your partner's suit.

10. Opening Shut-Out Bids

Expert bridge players make frequent use of "shut-out bids," also called pre-emptive bids, or more familiarly, "pre-empts." This is a very effective thing to do when you have a very long suit, particularly when your high-card strength is limited.

The length of your suit helps you to make tricks, provided that your suit becomes the trump suit. The height of your bid (usually for at least nine tricks) makes it difficult for the opponents to enter the bidding safely. Very often you succeed in shutting the opponents out of the bidding, even though they hold the majority of the high cards.

This style of bidding is fine for experienced partnerships, but is full of danger for beginners. Wait until you have played bridge for many months before you try any shut-out bids. You have many years of bridge-playing ahead of you, and there is lots of time for shut-out bidding.

When you think you are ready for it, or even earlier if you cannot resist temptation, here are the requirements for the opening shut-out bid of three or four in a suit:

An opening bid of three in a suit shows a seven-card or longer suit which cannot lose more than two tricks even against a very bad break. Your total strength in high cards should be less than 13 points. The total "playing strength" of the hand should be at least 6 tricks when you are not vulnerable; 7 tricks if you are vulnerable.

An opening bid of four in a suit shows *exactly the same type of hand except* that you have one trick more in playing strength. In other words, you should expect to develop seven tricks in the play if not vulnerable; eight tricks, vulnerable. In high card strength, you still have less than 13 points.

The "playing strength" of your hand is the number of tricks that can be won with that hand if you or your partner becomes declarer. It is usually easy to measure the playing strength of a hand that may be worth a shut-out bid because most of the tricks should come from a long and very strong trump suit.

In counting the trick-taking power of your trump suit, count the number of your trumps and then deduct one for each *high* trump (ace, king, or queen) that is missing from your hand. The remainder is the number of trump tricks that you can expect to win.

In counting the playing strength of your "side" suits (the suits that are not trumps), the general method is the same, but the result is not quite so reliable.

For example, suppose you hold K-Q-J-5 in a side suit. You count four cards in the suit, subtract one for the missing high card (the ace), and are left with a remainder of three. This is not a certainty, in the case of a relatively short suit; you may win only two tricks in that suit.

Your best procedure is to apply the same method to all suits but to remember that you are counting optimistically for your side suits. Be cautious about optimistic counts when you are vulnerable!

You are the dealer with each of the following hands. What should you say?

137.   ♠ Q J 10 9 7 6 3   ♥ 2   ♦ K Q J 5   ♣ 3

Bid four spades if not vulnerable but three spades if you are vulnerable. Your trump suit is of the right length and strength. You will have to give up two trump tricks, one to the ace and the other to the king, but then the remaining five tricks in the suit will be yours. You will also win two or three tricks in diamonds, so that the total trick-taking power of your hand is seven or eight tricks. That is exactly what you need for an opening bid of four spades when you are not vulnerable, but for safety's sake you should bid only three spades if you are vulnerable.

138. ♠ K 10 8 7 6 3 2 ♥ 2 ♦ K Q J 5 ♣ 3

Pass. Your spade suit is not strong enough for an opening shut-out bid. You might easily lose three or more tricks in the trump suit itself.

139. ♠ K Q J 10 9 7 5 ♥ 2 ♦ A Q J 5 ♣ 3

Bid one spade. Do not make a shut-out bid when you have 13 points or more in high cards.

11. Defensive Bidding

When one of the opponents has opened the bidding, it is usually wise for you to keep silent. It is seldom possible to make a game when one of the opponents has enough strength for an opening bid. If only a part-score is to be gained, you cannot afford to take big risks in the struggle for so small a prize.

Nevertheless, there are some reasons to enter the bidding "defensively." Your bid may indicate a favorable lead to your partner, in the event that an opponent becomes declarer. Sometimes, moreover, when the strength is fairly evenly divided between the two partnerships, you or your partner may become declarer at some safe part-score contract.

A safe defensive bid cannot be judged by the count of your points. It depends almost entirely on the *playing strength* of your hand.

DEFENSIVE OVERCALLS

Bid one in your strong suit (if you can legally do so) after the opponents have opened the bidding, provided that you have a strong suit of five cards or more and provided also that the hand will take four or five tricks even against pretty bad breaks.

Bid two when your suit is lower than the suit bid by the opponents, when you have an exceptionally strong suit of at least five cards and reasonable expectation of winning six tricks in the play of the cards.

South	West	North	East
1 ♥	?		

What do you, West, say with each of the following hands:

140.　♠ K Q J 7 3　♥ 5 2　♦ K 9 8 4　♣ 5 3

Bid one spade. You have a strong five-card suit, and can expect to win about four spades and a diamond even against fairly bad breaks.

141.　♠ 5 3　♥ 5 2　♦ K 9 8 4　♣ K Q J 7 3

Pass. The black suits have been exchanged, so that you must bid *two* clubs in order to overcall the opponent. The hand is not good for six playing tricks, and you therefore cannot bid at the level of two.

142.　♠ 5 3　♥ 5　♦ K 9 8 4　♣ K Q J 10 7 3

Bid two clubs. The hand contains six playing tricks—five in clubs and one in diamonds—and therefore may be bid at the level of two.

143.　♠ K Q J 7　♥ A 5 2　♦ K 9 8 4　♣ 5 3

Pass. Do not overcall on a four-card suit. You always need a strong suit of five or more cards for your overcall.

THE TAKEOUT DOUBLE

Sometimes an opponent will open the bidding and you will find that you have *very strong support for the other three suits,* without any special length in any of those suits. In such a situation you would be delighted to hear from your partner because you would be willing to raise any suit in which he happens to have length. In other words, you do not need strength from your partner, but merely an indication of which suit he has length in.

In one or two special situations you may obtain this information from your partner by means of the "takeout" double. This double asks your partner, "Take me out in (by bidding) your long suit, regardless of your strength." It does not have the normal meaning of a "business" double, which is that you expect to defeat the opponents and thus penalize them.

Naturally you will ask yourself a question at this moment: "How can my partner tell when I am doubling for a takeout and when I am doubling for business?"

That is a good question! Even experienced players sometimes have trouble on this point! In order to make it simple for you as a beginner, we will list the situations in which a double is meant for takeout:

	South	West	North	East
a.	1 ♥	Double		
b.	East	South	West	North
	Pass	1 ♥	Double	
c.	North	East	South	West
	Pass	Pass	1 ♥	Double
d.	North	East	South	West
	1 ♥	Pass	2 ♥	Double

In the first three cases West doubles a bid of one of a suit. In each of these cases this is West's first turn to act, and East has not yet bid.

In the fourth case West still makes his double at his first turn to act. This time, however, both of the opponents have spoken. Note especially that *East has not bid* but has merely passed.

This is a very important point. The purpose of the takeout double is to ask your partner to show the suit in which he has some length. If he has already shown his long suit by means of a bid, there is no need for you to make a takeout double. *If you double after your partner has bid a suit, your double is always for business* and not for takeout.

Note also that the takeout double is always made at your first chance to act. The bid that you are doubling is either one of a suit or two of a suit. *A double of any notrump bid is always a business double,* and so is a double of a bid of three or more in a suit.

REQUIREMENTS FOR A TAKEOUT DOUBLE

SHAPE: You need at least four-card support in any suit your partner may name. This kind of support in each of three suits accounts for twelve of your thirteen cards. Hence you can have only one card in the suit bid by the opponent. You may even be void in the suit bid by the opponent, in which case you should have five cards in one suit and four cards in each of the other two suits.

SIZE: You need at least 13 points in high cards for your takeout double. Ideally, your strength should be scattered through the three suits that you are ready to support. It is not fatal, however, if your strength is concentrated in only two of the three suits.

South	West	North	East
1 ♥	?		

What should you, West, do with each of the following hands?

144. ♠ K J 7 5   ♥ 3   ♦ K Q 9 4   ♣ A 6 3 2

Double. This is, of course, a takeout double. You have four-card support for any suit your partner may name, and you have a count of 13 points in high cards. This is the minimum requirement for a takeout double.

145. ♠ A J 7 5   ♥ 3   ♦ A Q 9 4   ♣ A K 3 2

Double. This is again a takeout double, but a much stronger one. You have four-card support for any suit your partner may name and you have a count of 18 points in high cards. This is five points more than the minimum expected by your partner.

146.　♠ K J 7 5　♥ 3　♦ Q J 9 4　♣ Q J 3 2

Pass. You have the right shape for a takeout double, but the wrong size. With only 10 points in high cards, you cannot afford to double.

147.　♠ K 7 5　♥ 3 2　♦ K Q 9 4　♣ A J 3 2

Pass. You have the right size for a takeout double, but the wrong shape. With this type of hand it is wiser to keep silent and let the opponents guess where the high cards are.

148.　♠ Q 5　♥ 3 2　♦ K Q 9　♣ A Q J 9 5 3

Bid two clubs. This is the right size for a takeout double, but decidedly the wrong shape. Since you have a very strong suit of your own, you can afford to bid it rather than pass.

RESPONDING TO A TAKEOUT DOUBLE

When your partner has doubled for a takeout, he has asked you to bid your longest suit. Note carefully that he has not asked about the suit in which you have strength but only about the suit in which you have length.

This does not mean that your partner is uninterested in the strength of your hand. The stronger your hand is, the better he will like it. However, your partner is especially interested in your *long suit* because that is the eventual trump suit.

Remember that your partner is sure to have at least four cards in the suit that you name. Remember also that he has a count of at least 13 points in high cards. Finally, remember that your partner has no more than a singleton in the suit bid by the opponents. Counting the value of his singleton as 2 points, your partner's hand is sure to count to at least 15 points, and it will usually count to more.

You can feel fairly confident of making a game when you have 10 or 11 points. The combined total will then be about 26 points.

You can have *some* hope for a game when you have a count of 8 or 9 points. There is still a chance that your partner will turn up with 17 or 18 points.

Your chance to make a game is not quite so good when you have fewer than 8 points. Nevertheless, no matter how weak your hand may be, you *must* respond to your partner's double. He has asked you to bid your longest suit, and you must not fail him.

CHOICE OF RESPONSE: If you have two four-card suits or two five-card suits, respond in the higher suit. If your only long suit has been bid by the opponents, your best course, usually, is to bid a minimum number of notrump.

THE PENALTY PASS: If you pass your partner's double, that double will be treated exactly as though it had been for penalties to begin with. You should do this only when you expect to penalize the opponents at their low contract. For this purpose you should have at least five cards in their suit, with such solidity that you are willing to lead trumps at every opportunity.

JUMP BIDS: You can confidently expect to make a game when your partner makes a takeout double and you have 10 points or more. In such a situation, make a jump bid in your best suit. If your best suit has been bid by the opponents, and if you have balanced distribution, you may make a jump response in notrump.

South	West	North	East
1 ♥	Double	Pass	?

What do you, East, say with each of the following hands:

149. ♠ 7 5 3 2 ♥ 9 3 2 ♦ 8 6 5 ♣ J 9 5

Bid one spade. You have a miserable hand, but do not let that bother you. West has a very good hand, and his strength will protect you from harm. Do not even dream of passing with this sort of hand: the weaker the hand, the more essential the takeout.

150.　♠ A Q 5 3 2　♥ 9 3　♦ 8 6 5　♣ J 9 5

Bid one spade. This is, of course, a far better hand than No. 149, but your response is still the same. If West takes any further action, you will try for a game.

151.　♠ A Q 5 3 2　♥ 9 3　♦ K 6 5　♣ J 9 5

Bid two spades. You have a count of 10 points and you must therefore show your strength by way of a jump response. This response is forcing until game is reached.

152.　♠ 5 3 2　♥ K J 3 2　♦ 8 6 5　♣ J 9 5

Bid one notrump. Your only length and strength are in the suit bid by the enemy. A minimum bid in notrump warns your partner of this fact. He will probably pass, and you will not be badly off at this low contract.

153.　♠ Q 3 2　♥ K J 3 2　♦ K 6 5　♣ J 9 5

Bid two notrump. You have a count of 10 points and must therefore show your strength by way of a jump response. Since you have no biddable suit in which to force, and since you have strength in the enemy's suit, you make your jump bid in notrump.

154.　♠ 3 2　♥ Q J 10 9 7　♦ 8 6 5　♣ J 9 5

Pass. If South plays the hand at hearts, you will probably win three trump tricks. Your partner's high cards should furnish enough side strength to defeat the contract. At any other contract your hand might well be quite worthless. Note the solidity of your hearts; with a less solid suit you would not pass for penalties.

REBIDDING BY THE DOUBLER

When you have doubled for a takeout you have already shown a hand with 13 points *in high cards*. Your partner will respond with a jump bid if he has 10 points or more, and then you will continue until game is reached.

If your partner responds without jumping, you know that he has fewer than 10 points. He may have a completely worthless hand, but he may have moderate strength up to about 9 points. Your task in rebidding is to stay out of trouble if he has a worthless hand but to reach a game if he has enough strength for that purpose.

When you have only 13 to 15 points in high cards, you may pass your partner's response (unless it is a jump response). Your partner has 9 points at best, and there is probably no game in the hand.

When you have 16 or 17 points in high cards, raise your partner's bid to the level of two. Thus, if your partner has been able to bid his suit at the level of one, you may raise it. If your partner's suit is lower than the enemy's, he has had to respond at the level of two; and in that case you merely pass.

When you have 18 or 19 points in high cards, you can get to the level of three. Raise your partner's suit to that level.

When you have 20 or 21 points in high cards, raise your partner's suit to game. There will usually be a sound play for this contract even when your partner has a very poor hand.

REBIDDING BY THE DOUBLER'S PARTNER

If you have 10 points or more, your first response is a jump bid, and you must thereafter keep bidding until a game is reached. This is usually no problem, since your partner will usually raise your suit, and then you can proceed as far as necessary to bid the game.

If you have made a non-jump response, wait to see what the doubler does next. You can tell how many points he has by the level of his next bid (if any), and then you can estimate the combined total.

Remember that your partner has a singleton that is worth about 2 points. Add that to the high cards shown by his rebid, and then add your own points. If the total is 26 (or even 25), proceed on to game. Otherwise let well enough alone.

South	West	North	East
1 ♥	Double	Pass	1 ♠
Pass	2 ♠	Pass	?

What do you, East, say with each of the following hands:

155. ♠ J 7 3 2 ♥ 9 3 2 ♦ K 8 4 ♣ J 6 2

Pass. You have a count of only 5 points, and your partner's bidding shows at most 17 points in high cards and 2 points for a singleton. The combined count is therefore only about 24 points, which will not give you a sound play for game.

156. ♠ J 7 3 2 ♥ 9 3 2 ♦ K 8 4 ♣ K 6 2

Bid three spades. You have a count of 7 points, and your partner has 16 or 17 points together with a singleton. Counting the singleton as 2 points, the combined count is 25 or 26 points.

157. ♠ J 8 7 3 2 ♥ 9 3 2 ♦ K 4 ♣ K 6 2

Bid four spades. This is the same as hand No. 156 except that you now have a five-card spade suit. The extra trump is enough to tip the balance in favor of an immediate game bid.

COMPETITIVE BIDDING

When both sides bid in competition with each other, there is reason to believe that the strength is fairly equally divided. Be cautious about bidding a game, and be even more cautious about considering a slam.

This caution applies to lower-than-game bids also. Suppose your partner opens and your right-hand opponent makes a bid before you get a chance to respond. When both sides are in the bidding you can afford to pass any "borderline" bid. Your partner will have a chance to bid; and if he likewise prefers to pass, you are both better off letting the opponents play the hand.

If you do decide to bid right after an opponent's bid, your decision shows that you have good values for your bid. For example, suppose your partner opens the bidding with one spade. You may raise to two spades with 6 to 10 points (provided that your hand includes proper trump support). If the player at your right bids two hearts, however, you can afford to pass a 6-point or 7-point hand. Your raise to two spades in this situation should show at least 8 points.

The same sort of caution applies to bidding your own suit. For example, suppose you have a club suit with a count of 10 points. Your partner opens with one spade, and you plan to respond with two clubs. But the next player bids two hearts, and you must now think of bidding *three clubs*. Better not when you have only 10 points, since your minimum requirement for showing a lower suit is 9 points. You can't feel that you have solid values until you have at least 11 points. Consider a raise of partner's spades, or even a pass.

SACRIFICE BIDDING

When both sides are competing during the bidding, it is often difficult to discover which side can make its contract. As a general rule, stop bidding when you think you have come to the end of your strength. You will be pleasantly surprised to learn how often the opponents fail to make their contract when they outbid you!

On rare occasions the opponents will bid a game when you have a long, strong suit that your partner has supported. If the opponents are dependable bidders, you may well believe that they can make their game contract. At the same time you may believe that you will be set only one or two tricks if you outbid them at your own suit. In that case, go ahead and outbid them as a sacrifice measure.

Note all the precautions that you must take to make sure that this procedure is sound. Don't bother to outbid undependable opponents: they may be "overboard," and your sacrifice bid will throw them a lifeline. Don't make a sacrifice bid without a very strong and long suit that has been raised by your partner: no disaster can overwhelm you when the trump suit is strong and when your partner has a little something.

PENALTY DOUBLES

Double the opponents when they step out of line. This will cure them of the habit of outrageous overbidding.

Do not double, however, merely because the opponents have bid to a high level. Experienced opponents will not climb so high without a good reason, and they will be quick to redouble if you double on mere suspicion.

There is no easy guide to penalty doubles, because the best procedure varies according to your hand, the way the bidding has gone, and the skill of the opponents. A good general rule to follow is: Don't double when you expect to set the enemy only one trick. Double only when you expect to set them two tricks or more.

For example, suppose the opponents have climbed up to a contract of four spades. You can see four probable defensive tricks in your hand. Do not double. Those four tricks will set the opponents only one. Wait until you can reasonably expect a two-trick set before you double.

This may sound unreasonable, but there is a good reason for this advice. Four probable tricks have a way of becoming only three actual tricks when the hand is played. You need that extra defensive trick as a safety margin.

Another reason for caution is that your double may tell declarer where the high cards are, and he may find a way to make his contract that he would never attempt if you had merely passed. Surprise is often half of your strength, and it is foolish to give up this important weapon.

One other pointer about doubles: Do not double a trump contract unless you have at least one sure trump trick. Too many weird things happen when you double without trump strength.

REDOUBLES

Don't!

There is such a thing as a good redouble, but not for a beginner. When you have gained quite a bit of experience, you can redouble a contract that you feel confident about—provided that you can punish the enemy if they try to escape from the redouble by means of a sacrifice bid. At the beginning, however, you cannot feel so confident about any contract.

12. The Play Of The Hand

The most helpful way to learn the fundamentals of bridge play is by actual play. Provide yourself with a deck of cards, and as you read each example, lay out the cards on the table exactly as the diagram indicates. Then proceed to play out the cards as you read, and you will soon get the "feel" of the cards, as well as the understanding of why each play is made.

PLAYING A SINGLE SUIT

As you know, there are four suits in the complete deck of cards. If you learn how to get the most out of each suit, you will be able to play a complete hand in such a way as to get the largest possible number of tricks out of it.

Your first step in learning the play of the cards, therefore, is to concentrate on a single suit. Of course, if you hold in one hand all the top cards of a suit, you will play them out one at a time and win a trick with each. In the event that your "honors are split" between your hand and your partner's (or dummy) you will be faced with problems requiring thought and practice.

Let's see what may happen.

Take all thirteen spades from a deck of cards. For the rest of this section we are going to forget about the other three suits and we are going to play as though spades were our only problem.

You are South in each of the diagrams of this chapter. The North hand is the dummy, and the East-West players are the defenders. Sit at a table with South's spades in your own hand, and North's spades across the table from you as part of a dummy hand. We will refer to the dummy as North and you (South) will play out the cards from dummy when it is North's turn to play.

1.
                    North (dummy)
                    ♠ K 2
          West   East
                    South
                    ♠ A Q 5

Let's suppose that you begin by leading the ace of spades from the South hand. West follows suit with any small spade, dummy follows suit with the deuce of spades, and East follows suit with a low spade. The ace of spades wins that trick and the lead remains in the South hand.

You now wish to continue the suit. Which card do you lead, the queen or the five?

The only play now is to lead the five of spades. The reason is that the North hand must follow suit with the king of spades. It would be a shame to waste your own queen on North's king! Therefore you lead the five of spades at the second trick and save your queen to be used later on.

As in the first trick, East and West follow suit with low spades. North's king wins the second trick in the suit.

What has happened? North is now out of spades. South would like to win a trick with his queen of spades, but he does not have the right to lead at this moment. North has won the previous trick, and therefore North must lead to the next trick. If South wishes to win a trick with his queen of spades, he must win some other trick in his own hand before he can lead that good queen of spades.

What happens if South is unable to win any further trick

in his own hand? In that case, he will never be able to win a trick with his queen of spades. This will mean that South will win only two spade tricks in spite of the fact that he began with the three top cards in the suit.

This sort of difficulty can be avoided if South merely wins his tricks in the correct order!

Notice that South has three spades, while North has only two spades. For this reason, South is the "long" hand, and North is the "short" hand. In general, it is correct to win the first trick in the *short* hand rather than in the *long* hand.

South should begin by leading the five of spades to North's king of spades. The opponents follow suit with low spades, and North's king wins the first trick in the suit.

Notice this carefully. Although the ace is the highest card of the suit, it isn't necessary for the ace to win the first trick. The player who holds the ace (in this case South) may be willing to play a small card and let some other card win the first trick.

After winning the first spade trick with the king, North is on lead and leads his remaining spade, the deuce.

Now South can win the second spade trick with his ace. The two opponents follow suit with low spades, and South has the right to lead to the third trick. This gives South his chance to lead the queen of spades and win a third trick in the suit.

Why are we able to win only two tricks in the first case but three tricks when we play the suit properly? The secret lies in beginning the suit by *"playing high from the short hand."*

2.

North
♠ A 2

West   East

South
♠ K Q 5

Here we see almost exactly the same situation. The only difference is that the ace and king have been exchanged.

The *correct* method is to win the first trick in the *short* hand. This means that North must win the first spade trick with the ace. North can then lead the remaining spade, the deuce, and South can win the second spade trick with the king. This leaves him in his own hand, so that he has the right to lead the queen of spades and thus win a third trick in the suit.

3.

North
♠ K 2

West   East

South
♠ Q J 5

This is a similar situation, except that the ace of spades is now held by one of the opponents. Our problem, therefore, is to win two out of the three possible spade tricks.

The procedure is much the same. We cannot be sure of *winning* the first trick in the short hand, since the opponent who holds the ace of spades may decide to take his ace at that moment. We can, however, begin by playing a high card from the short hand.

In other words, we begin the spade suit by playing the king from the North hand. If the North hand happens to be in the lead, we simply lead the king of spades. If the South hand happens to be in the lead, we lead the five of spades and play the king of spades from the North hand.

The first trick "drives out" the ace of spades. This gives one of the opponents the right to lead to the next trick, to be sure. If we are able to win a trick later on, however, we will then be in position to take the second spade trick with the queen. After winning a trick with the queen of spades, we will also be able to win another trick with the jack.

Notice how different it is if you begin the wrong way, by leading a high card from the long hand instead of from the short hand. For example, suppose you begin the spades by leading the queen of spades from the South hand. The deuce of spades is played from the North hand, and one of the opponents takes the trick with the ace of spades.

When you win a different trick later on, you are able to lead the five of spades to North's king of spades. Now, however, you are not in position to take the third trick in the suit. You are in the North hand, and the third spade trick can be won only if you are in position to lead from the South hand.

While we're at it, let's notice something else about the play of the spades in this example. We would normally expect the ace to win the first trick of any suit; the king to win the second; the queen to win the third, and so on. In this example, however, the king and the ace are both played to the first trick. This "promotes" the queen so that it can win the second trick of the suit. In the same way, the jack is promoted so that it can win the third trick in the suit.

This is like what may happen in a battle. If the general gets killed in a battle, the colonel takes his place and everybody else moves up one step. If several officers are killed, a young lieutenant may find himself commanding the regiment. In bridge, likewise, several high cards may fall on the same trick, thus leaving a lowly jack or ten in command of the suit.

4.
               North
               ♠ Q 2
West   East
               South
               ♠ K J 5

Here we see a similar situation, except that the queen and king of spades have been exchanged. The procedure is still the same.

We must begin by playing a high card from the short hand. If North has won the previous trick, the queen of spades is led from the North hand. If South has won the previous trick, the five of spades is led from the South hand, and the queen of spades is played from the North hand. The ace of spades is thus driven out, and South is ready to win the next *two* spade tricks as soon as he can win a trick and thus gain the lead.

5.
> **North**
> ♠ Q 2

West   **East**

> **South**
> ♠ A K 5 4 3

The situation is once more similar, except that this time South has a *long* spade suit. The suit is still properly begun by winning the first trick in the short hand. This makes it easy to continue the suit.

THE FINESSE

One of the most important plays in bridge is known as the "finesse." This play is most easily explained by example.

6.
> **North**
> ♠ 3 2

West   **East**
♠ 5 4   ♠ K 6

> **South**
> ♠ A Q

Let's suppose, to begin with, that South has the lead. He leads the ace of spades, and each of the other players follows suit with a low spade. This leaves East in command of the situation with his king of spades. Whenever the suit is led again, East will be able to win a trick with his king.

Is South better off if he begins the spades by leading the queen from his own hand? Not at all. Instead of playing the six of spades, East will play his king and will thus win the first spade trick.

It is therefore clear that South must lose one spade trick if he begins by leading the suit from his own hand. It doesn't matter whether he leads the ace first and the queen next, or vice versa. In either case, East will play his low spade on the ace and his king of spades on the queen.

The situation is very different if you begin the spade suit by leading a spade from the North hand. It is East's turn to play next, and he may play either the six of spades or the king of spades.

If East plays the king of spades, South will play the ace and win the trick. Having thus captured the king of spades, South is in position to lead the queen of spades and win a trick with it.

What happens if East plays the six of spades at the first trick instead of the king? South now "takes a finesse" by playing the queen of spades. West has to follow suit with a low spade, thus completing the trick with a fourth card. South's queen of spades is the highest in the trick, and therefore wins the trick.

Notice that South is able to win a trick with the queen of spades even though an opponent has a higher spade (the king). The reason is that South doesn't have to choose his own play until East has already played. Once East has put the six of spades down on the table, of course, he cannot pick it up and substitute the king for it. South can therefore win a trick by "finessing the queen of spades."

7.

	North	
	♠ 3 2	
West		East
♠ K 6		♠ 5 4
	South	
	♠ A Q	

A finesse doesn't always succeed. In this diagram we have reversed the cards held by East and West. A low spade is led from the North hand, and East plays low. Now it is West who can choose his play after South has already played. If South puts the ace of spades down on the table, West will play his low spade and will save his king to win the next trick. If South tries a finesse by playing the queen, West will win the trick immediately by playing his king.

When you are actually playing a hand, you do not know which cards are held by West and which cards are held by East. Sometimes a missing king will be in the East hand, and sometimes it will be in the West hand. Roughly speaking, the king will be at your left about half of the time and at your right the other half of the time.

This means that your finesse will succeed about half of the time and will fail the other half of the time. Don't be discouraged by the failures. When a finesse succeeds you have manufactured a trick out of thin air. When it loses, you have given the opponents only what belonged to them anyway!

8.
$$\begin{array}{ccc} & \text{North} & \\ & \spadesuit\ 3\ 2 & \\ \text{West} & & \text{East} \\ \spadesuit\ 6\ 5 & & \spadesuit\ A\ Q \\ & \text{South} & \\ & \spadesuit\ K\ 4 & \end{array}$$

Not all finesses involve the ace and queen of the suit. In this diagram you have the king of spades, and your problem is to win a trick with it.

Suppose, to begin with, that the lead is in the South hand. If you lead the king of spades, East will play the ace and will thus win the trick. East will also win the second spade trick with his queen.

Can you do any better by leading your low spade instead of the king of spades? No. When you lead your low spade, East will win the trick with his queen, thus saving the ace of spades to win a trick later on.

In short, you must surely lose both spade tricks if the lead is in the South hand.

The situation is different if the lead is in the North hand. You begin the suit by leading the deuce of spades.

If East plays his ace of spades, you are able to play the four of spades from the South hand. The next time spades are led, your king will win the trick.

If East plays the queen instead of the ace, you will play your king at the first trick. West will have to play a low spade, and your king will win at once.

In other words, you are able to win a trick with your king of spades provided that you lead the suit first from the North hand. It doesn't matter whether East plays his ace on the first trick or on the second trick. Either way, your king will win a trick when you lead towards it.

Now let us exchange the East and West hands. This puts the ace-queen of spades in the West hand.

Whenever you play your king of spades, West will capture the trick with his ace. Whenever you play the low spade from your hand, West be able to win the trick with the queen. This is equally true whether you lead from your own hand or from the North hand.

In short, you can win a spade trick if you lead the suit first from the North hand, provided that *East* has the ace. This will be true about half the time. Hence if you begin the suit correctly you have a fifty-fifty chance to win a trick in it.

9.
      North
      ♠ 3 2

West   East
♠ A 4   ♠ Q 5

      South
      ♠ K J

Our next finessing position is more complicated than those we have examined up to this time. South will not win any spade tricks at all if he begins the suit from his own hand. For example, if South begins by leading the king of spades, West will take the ace. This will leave East with the queen of spades, which will win the second trick in that suit.

South can gain nothing by first leading the jack of spades from his own hand. In this case, West will play low, and East will win the first trick with the queen of spades. Now West will be able to win the second spade trick with his ace.

As in all the previous examples, the correct play is to begin the suit with a lead from the North hand. *The general rule is to lead a suit from a weak holding towards a strong holding.*

When North leads the deuce of spades, East may play either the queen or the five.

If East plays the queen of spades, South can "cover" with the king of spades. South is now sure of a spade trick. If West takes the ace, South's jack will be good for the second trick in the suit. If West plays a low spade on the first trick, South wins that trick immediately with his king.

What happens if East plays the five of spades on the first trick of the suit? South must finesse the jack. If West wants to win the trick, he must play his ace. This will leave South in command of the suit with his king. If West does not play the ace, South wins the first spade trick with his jack!

Now exchange the East and West hands. West now has the queen and five of spades, while East has the ace and four of spades. South can still gain nothing by leading the suit from his own hand. Regardless of the position of the cards, the opponent who has the ace will take the trick whenever South leads the king; and the opponent who has the queen of spades will play it whenever South leads the jack of spades. Either way, South must lose both tricks in the suit.

The proper procedure is to lead the deuce of spades from the North hand at the first trick. East plays low, and South must decide whether to play the king or the jack.

When the cards are in their new position, South can win a spade trick only by playing the king at this moment. West will be obliged to play a low spade, and the king of spades will win.

If South tries to finesse the jack of spades, West will win with the queen of spades. Later on, East's ace of spades will win the other trick in the suit.

The question is: How does South know whether to play the king or the jack of spades at the first trick? The answer is that he *doesn't* know. He must guess!

Even a guess is better than nothing. No matter how unlucky South may be, he will sometimes guess right. When he does, he will win one spade trick. If South simply surrenders and leads the spades from his own hand, he will *never* win a spade trick.

You will meet many such "guess" situations as you play bridge. Your best course is to make your guess quickly and then carry on with the rest of the play. If you take forever to make up your mind, you will bore all of the players and will become unpopular. Moreover, no matter how long you take about it, your chance to guess right doesn't become better!

10.

North
♠ 4 3 2

West   East
♠ A 10 9   ♠ K 8 7

South
♠ Q J 5

We see here still another finesse situation. South can win a spade trick if he is patient enough and if North can keep regaining the lead by winning tricks in other suits.

The correct procedure is to lead the first spade from the North hand. East plays a low spade, and South plays the queen. West must play the ace of spades to win this trick, since otherwise South would win his spade trick immediately with the queen.

In a regular hand, West would now lead some other suit, and it would be important for North to win the trick in order to lead another spade. When the next spade is led, East may play either the king or the eight. If East plays the king, South plays the low spade and will have the jack of spades to win a spade trick later on. If East plays the eight of spades, South wins the trick immediately by playing the jack.

Notice that South will not win a spade trick if he begins the suit by leading it from his own hand.

11.
                        North
                        ♠ 4 3 2
    West   East
    ♠ A 9 8   ♠ K J 7
                        South
                        ♠ Q 10 5

This situation is very similar to the last case. South can win a spade trick only by leading the suit twice from the North hand.

When North leads a low spade, East may play the king, the jack, or the seven. No play will stop South from winning a trick.

If East plays the king, he wins the trick. Later on, North regains the lead and leads another spade. This time East may play either the jack or the seven. If East plays the jack, South covers with the queen; and if East plays the seven, South finesses the ten. In either case, West's ace is driven out, and South is left with the highest spade.

12.
                        North
                        ♠ 4 3 2
    West   East
    ♠ 8 7 6   ♠ K 10 9
                        South
                        ♠ A Q J

Here we see an example of a "continued finesse." South

must lead the suit first from the North hand in order to finesse the queen. This finesse succeeds because the king of spades is in the favorable position.

South must now lead a different suit from his hand in order to get the lead back in the North hand. This permits him to lead a second spade from the North hand through East's king. South now finesses the jack of spades, winning that trick also. There is nothing that East can do to save himself, for if he ever plays the king of spades, South will pounce on the trick with the ace of spades.

13.
```
                        North
                        ♠ 4 3 2
     West                              East
     ♠ A 9 8                           ♠ Q 7 6
                        South
                        ♠ K J 10
```

Here we have another continued finesse. North begins the suit by leading the deuce, East plays low, and South finesses the jack. This play drives out West's ace.

Now South must win a trick in some different suit in the North hand. This enables North to lead another spade through East's queen. If East plays low, South finesses the ten, thus winning the trick. South is sure to win two spade tricks by this maneuver; if East ever plays the queen of spades South can cover with the king.

14.
```
                        North
                        ♠ 4 3 2
     West                              East
     ♠ 8 7 6                           ♠ K J 9
                        South
                        ♠ A Q 10
```

Here we see an example of the "double finesse." North leads the deuce of spades, and East's cards are trapped. No matter what East does, South will win the trick as cheaply as possible with a finesse.

For example, if East plays the nine, South will cover with the ten of spades and win that trick. If East plays the jack of spades, South will cover with the queen of spades and win the finesse in that way. Nor does it do East any good to play the king of spades, for then South would win the trick with the ace.

Having won the first finesse, South gets back to the North hand by way of a different suit. This enables him to lead another spade through East. Once again, South is able to take a finesse by barely covering whichever card East plays.

Note that South must not finesse the queen on the first trick if East plays the nine. If South makes this mistake, East will be left with the king-jack of spades, while South has the ace-ten. There can be no finesse in this situation, and East is sure to win one spade trick with his king or with his jack.

Just for the sake of variation, exchange the jack and the eight of spades. This will give us a position in which one finesse wins, while the other loses.

You begin the suit, as always, by leading from the North hand. East plays low, and you finesse the ten. In the new position, West is able to win this trick with the jack. Later on, you must lead the spades again from the North hand and this time your finesse of the queen will succeed.

You might exchange the king and the eight of spades instead of the jack and eight. This time your first finesse of the ten of spades would drive out the king. The ace and queen would then be high, and no further finesse would be necessary.

There is still one remaining possibility. West may have both the king and the jack of spades. In this position, both finesses lose, and you make only one spade trick (the ace).

How do you know which finesses will win and which finesses will lose? The answer is that you *don't* know. It usually costs you nothing to try the finesse, in the hope that it will succeed.

15.

North
♠ 4 3 2

West   East
♠ K 9 8   ♠ Q 7 6

South
♠ A J 10

Here we have a different example of the double finesse. South's problem is to win two out of the three spade tricks.

The suit is begun by a lead from the North hand. East plays low, and South finesses the jack. This drives out West's king. North must then regain the lead in a different suit and lead another spade. Now South is in position to finesse the ten of spades, thus winning two spade tricks.

The position would amount to the same thing if the king and queen of spades were exchanged. The finesse of the jack would then lose to the queen, but the second finesse (of the ten of spades) would succeed.

What happens if East has both the king and the queen of spades? He must play one of his high cards at the first trick, since otherwise South will win the first spade trick by finessing the jack.

When East plays the queen of spades at the first trick, South wins with the ace. South can now return the jack of spades to drive out the king. The ten of spades will then be good to win the third trick in the suit.

What happens if *West* has both the king and the queen of spades? In this case South loses both of the finesses. He wins only one spade trick, with the ace.

16.

North
♠ 4 3 2

West   East
♠ 8 7 6   ♠ Q J 9

South
♠ A K 10

This is still another example of the double finesse. North leads a low spade, and East must decide whether to play low or to "split his equals." If East plays low, South wins a finesse immediately with the ten of spades, thus making sure of all three tricks in the suit.

If East splits his equals by putting up the jack, South wins with the king. South must next return to dummy by way of a different suit in order to lead another spade. Now East's queen is trapped. If East plays low, South wins a trick with the ten; if East plays the queen, South wins with the ace and then can win the next trick with the ten.

Note that this double finesse can succeed only if East has both the queen and the jack. If one of these cards is held by West (or if both are held by West) the finesse loses, and South makes only his ace and king.

17.
                        North
                        ♠ Q J 9
        West   East
        ♠ 10 6 3   ♠ K 8 7
                        South
                        ♠ A 5 4

Sometimes the high cards needed for a finesse are scattered between your hand and the dummy. In this case, North has some of the high cards.

You must begin the suit by leading the queen from the North hand. East should play a low spade, and you must allow the queen to "ride" for a finesse. That is, you do not cover it. The queen wins the trick, and you are thus sure of two spade tricks, as you still have the ace.

Two tricks are all you can win against this correct defense. If North continues by leading the jack of spades on the second round of the suit, East will cover with the king. You can win that trick with the ace, but then West controls the third trick in the suit with his ten.

If you lead the *nine* of spades from the North hand at the second trick, East plays low, and you must play the ace from your own hand to prevent West from winning with the ten. This will leave the king of spades in the East hand to win the third trick.

Incorrect defense by East would enable you to win all three spade tricks! For example, East might mistakenly play the king of spades on the first trick when North led the queen.

You would then win with the ace of spades and return the suit from your own hand. Dummy's jack-nine would then give you a finessing position over West's ten. For example, if West plays the six of spades on the second trick, North could then win a finesse by playing the nine of spades.

The general rule for the defenders (East and West) is *not* to cover the queen when dummy also has the jack.

18.

North

♠ Q 5 4

West   East

♠ 10 6 3   ♠ K 8 7

South

♠ A J 9

If North begins by leading the queen, East must cover with the king. South wins with the ace of spades and returns to dummy with another suit in order to try a second spade lead from the North hand. He now finesses the nine of spades, but this finesse loses to West's ten. South therefore wins only two spade tricks.

South would win all three spade tricks against incorrect defense. For example, suppose that East failed to cover with the king when North began the suit by leading the queen. The queen would be allowed to ride as a finesse, and it would win the trick. Dummy would still be in the lead, and would immediately lead another spade. Now South could win a finesse with the jack.

The rule for the defenders in this case is *to cover the queen with the king when dummy does not also hold the jack.*

Let us repeat both of these rules because you will often meet these situations when you are defending. When dummy has *two or more honors in sequence,* you do *not* cover the honor that is led through you for a finesse. When dummy has *only one honor* and leads that honor through you for a finesse, you *do* cover.

19.

$$\begin{array}{c} \text{North} \\ \spadesuit \ Q \ 3 \ 2 \end{array}$$

$$\begin{array}{ccc} \text{West} & & \text{East} \\ \spadesuit \ K \ 8 \ 7 & & \spadesuit \ J \ 10 \ 9 \end{array}$$

$$\begin{array}{c} \text{South} \\ \spadesuit \ A \ 5 \ 4 \end{array}$$

The new position looks something like the old one, but there is an important difference. You must not begin the suit by leading the queen from the North hand.

If you do, West wins that first trick with his king. You will win only your ace of spades. You are no better off if the king of spades happens to be in the East hand. East covers the queen with the king of spades, thus driving out your ace. You cannot then hope to win a second spade trick with any other card.

The correct play of the suit is to win a trick first with the ace of spades then lead a low spade towards North's queen. If West plays the king on the second round of the suit, North will win the third spade trick with the queen. If West plays low on the second round of the suit, North's queen wins the second trick immediately.

Like other finessing positions, this is not sure-fire. If the king of spades happens to be in the East hand, North's queen will not win a trick.

20.
North
♠ 4 3 2

West   East
♠ 8 7 6   ♠ Q 10 9

South
♠ A K J

Here we have a simple finesse again. The suit is begun from the dummy. North leads a low spade, and South finesses the jack. The finesse succeeds because East has the queen of spades.

We can now add one extra refinement to the play of this combination of cards. South should not begin the suit by taking a finesse. Instead he should lead the ace of spades first. There is a slim possibility that West has the singleton queen of spades. If so, the queen will drop when the ace is led, and no finesse will be needed.

If the queen does not drop on the first trick, you must enter the dummy with some different suit and then lead a spade in order to finesse the jack. The preliminary play of taking the ace of spades costs nothing and may save you from losing to a singleton queen.

PLAYING FOR A DROP

21.
North
♠ 3 2

West   East
♠ 6 5 4   ♠ J 9 8 7

South
♠ A K Q 10

In this situation your object is to win all four spade tricks. One way of playing the suit is to lead the ace, the king, and the queen in the hope that one of them will "drop" the jack. If so, your ten will then be good for the fourth trick.

Another way of playing the suit is to take a finesse. If you decide to finesse, you should nevertheless take the first trick with the ace, get to North by way of some different suit, and then lead a low spade and finesse the ten.

22.

	North	
	♠ 5 4 3 2	
West		East
♠ J 9 8		♠ 7 6
	South	
	♠ A K Q 10	

The situation is much the same, except that this time you have eight spades between your own hand and the dummy. There are only five spades missing, and the most even division of those five spades is three in one hand and two in the other. That is what you should expect.

If you win the first three spade tricks with the ace, the king, and the queen, the opponents will be obliged to follow suit. The player who has the jack of spades will have to follow suit with it on one of those first three tricks. When he has done so, the ten of spades becomes "high" or "established." This means that the ten of spades will win a spade trick whenever it is led.

Compare this with a *finesse* in spades. If you lead a spade from the North hand and finesse the ten from the South hand, it will lose to West's jack.

If you play to *drop* the jack of spades by leading out the ace, king, and queen, you will win all four tricks. Obviously, the play for the drop is better in this case than the finesse. In the previous case, however, the finesse was better than the play for the drop.

CHOOSING BETWEEN A DROP AND FINESSE

When should you finesse, and when should you play for the drop? There are just a few very common situations where this choice arises. Let's examine the most important of these situations.

23.
North
♠ 5 4 3 2

West   East

South
♠ A Q J 7 6

You lead a spade from the North hand, and East follows suit with a low spade. Should you finesse the queen, or should you play the ace in the hope that the king will drop on it?

The opponents have four spades between them. The opponent who has the king of spades is assumed to have half of the four spades, or two altogether. He will not have to play his king on your ace, so the play for the drop will not work. Therefore you try a finesse.

It would still be correct to finesse even if you had one additional spade, leaving only three spades to be shared by the opponents. *You play to drop a king only when you have a total of eleven cards in the suit between your own hand and the dummy.*

24.
North
♠ 5 4 3 2

West   East

South
♠ A K J 7 6

The situation is the same except that the missing honor is the queen this time instead of the king. Each opponent should have two spades, and in that case you can capture them all by leading out your ace and then your king. Hence the play for the drop is better than the finesse.

25.
North
♠ 4 3 2

West   East

South
♠ A K J 7 6

The missing honor is still the queen, but this time the opponents have five spades between them instead of only four. You assume that the opponent who has the queen has the larger "half"—or a total of three spades. He will not be forced to play his queen when you lead out your ace and king. Hence you try a finesse.

Let's boil this down to a rule. *You do not finesse for a queen* when you have *nine or more* cards of a suit between your own hand and the dummy. *You do finesse for a queen* when you have *eight or fewer* cards of a suit between your own hand and the dummy. In the old days this finessing rule used to be expressed thus: "With nine, never; with eight, ever."

ESTABLISHING A SUIT

When the high cards of a suit have been played, one or two low cards often remain. Those low cards are said to be "established" because they will win tricks when led (provided that nobody can trump them).

26.
     North
     ♠ 8 7 6

West   East
♠ J 10 9   ♠ 5 4

     South
     ♠ A K Q 3 2

South leads the ace of spades, winning the first trick. He continues with the king of spades, and then with the queen. Each time West must follow suit with a spade, so that his nine, ten, and jack fall uselessly on South's ace, king, and queen.

After the first three tricks the only spades left unplayed are South's three and deuce. Those are "established." When South leads them, nobody can play a higher spade.

Sometimes it is possible to establish a long suit even though you don't hold any high cards to begin with. For example:

27.

North
♠ 5 4

West　　　　　　　　　　　　　**East**
♠ J 10 9　　　　　　　　　　　♠ A K Q

South
♠ 8 7 6 3 2

East can take the first three spade tricks. When he has done so, however, South's remaining spades will be established.

Why should East do South such a favor? Very often he will not do it willingly. South may have to lead spades three times to drive out East's high cards. This means that South must be able to win several tricks in the other suits so that he can have the right to lead spades.

28.

North
♠ 5 4

West　　　　　　　　　　　　　**East**
♠ 8 7 6　　　　　　　　　　　♠ K 10 9

South
♠ A Q J 3 2

South wants to establish the spade suit. He leads the first spade from the North hand in order to finesse the queen. That play succeeds, so South must get back to dummy by winning a trick in a different suit in the North hand. North leads the other spade, and South finesses the jack.

After taking two successful finesses South *must* play to drop the king by leading his ace. This is not a matter of rule; South has just run out of finesses, and now the play for the drop is all that he has left!

As it happens, the king does drop, and South's two low spades become established. If the king had not dropped on the third trick, (for example, put the eight of spades in the East hand), South would merely give up the fourth trick in the suit by leading a low spade. This would establish South's fifth spade.

Let us sum up suit establishment. If you have high cards in your long suit, you try to win tricks with those high cards in the normal way: You may play for a drop, you may try a finesse, or you may give up one high card to promote another.

After you have made all the normal high-card plays, your low cards will usually be established. If they are still not good, you may have to lead a low card and give up a trick in order to set up your remaining low cards.

In rare cases, you will have no high cards in your long suit. You will simply lead the suit, allowing the opponents to take their top cards. After they have done so, your remaining cards in the suit will be good.

Suit establishment is important because in most hands five or six tricks are won by low cards. You must know how to "bring up" your low cards so that they will win tricks for you when they have grown up.

RUFFING

Ruffing is not a single-suit play, because it requires two suits. You lead a side suit from your own hand, and you play a trump from the dummy; or you may lead a side suit from the dummy and play a trump from your own hand. This is called "ruffing."

The play is possible, of course, only when the hand that ruffs has no cards in the side suit.

29.
<pre>
                         North
                         ♠ 4 3 2
                         ♥ None
        West   East
        ♠ 9 8 7   ♠ 6 5
        ♥ A K J 9 8   ♥ Q 10 7 6 5
                         South
                         ♠ A K Q J 10
                         ♥ 4 3 2
</pre>

Spades are trumps, and South has the lead. His problem is to avoid losing those three tiny hearts.

He leads a heart from his hand and plays a trump from the dummy. This wins the trick. That is his first ruffing trick.

Now South would like to return to his own hand in order to do the same thing all over again. How does he get back to the South hand?

Ideally, he would lead some entirely different suit from the North hand and win the trick in the South hand. Then he could lead a second heart and ruff it in the dummy. Ideally, to continue, he would again get back to the South hand by winning a diamond or a club, and lead his last heart to ruff it with dummy's last low trump.

Suppose that South is unable to win any trick in clubs or diamonds? Then, after ruffing the first heart in the North hand, he must return to his own hand with a trump.

This is far from ideal, because it uses up one of dummy's precious low trumps. South can then ruff a second low heart in the North hand, but that will use up the last of dummy's three trumps. The last low heart in the South hand must eventually be given up to the enemy, unless South can work out some other way to avoid the loss of the trick.

30.
<pre>
                    North
                    ♠ 4 3 2
                    ♥ 5
      West   East
      ♠ 9 8 7   ♠ 6 5
      ♥ A K J 9 8   ♥ Q 10 7 6
                    South
                    ♠ A K Q J 10
                    ♥ 4 3 2
</pre>

South would like to ruff his losing hearts in the dummy, but cannot do so while dummy still has a heart. South must lead a heart and allow the opponents to win one trick in that suit. This will remove the singleton heart from the dummy, after which South will be able to lead hearts from his own hand and ruff in the North hand.

The opponents, if they are wise, will lead back a trump when they are given their heart trick. Their object is to remove trumps from the dummy, which will prevent declarer (South) from ruffing in the dummy.

31.

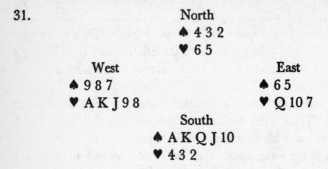

North
♠ 4 3 2
♥ 6 5

West
♠ 9 8 7
♥ A K J 9 8

East
♠ 6 5
♥ Q 10 7

South
♠ A K Q J 10
♥ 4 3 2

South would like to ruff a heart in dummy. Before he can do so he must remove both of dummy's hearts.

South begins by leading a low heart, allowing the enemy to win the trick. They return a trump, and South wins with the ten of spades.

South next leads a second heart, giving up that trick also. Once again a trump is led back, and South wins with the jack of spades.

South can now lead his last heart and trump with dummy's last spade. The trick has been produced, but it was hard work!

It should be evident that it was easiest to produce the ruffing tricks when North was *void* of hearts. It was still fairly easy to do so when North had a *singleton* heart. It was difficult to do so when North had a *doubleton* heart.

Think back to your point count. During the bidding you counted 3 points for a void, 2 points for a singleton, and only

1 point for a doubleton. The difference in point value is caused by this very difference in their *playing* value.

DISCARDING

Discarding is a three-suit play. In the example, we needn't worry about the cards held by East and West.

32.
                  North
                  ♠ 4 3 2
                  ♥ 7 6 5
                  ♦ A K Q

West   East

                  South
               ♠ A K Q J 10
               ♥ 4 3 2
               ♦ 2

If hearts were led immediately, South would lose three tricks in that suit. Fortunately, South has the lead, and he does not intend to lead a heart.

Instead, South leads his deuce of diamonds. Dummy wins with the ace and continues the suit by leading the king of diamonds. South cannot follow suit on this trick, so he *discards* the deuce of hearts. In this way South eliminates a losing card from his hand.

The process continues. North next leads the queen of diamonds, which is good for another trick. South discards the three of hearts, thus eliminating a second losing card from his hand.

Up to this point only two suits have been involved. Discards are most useful, however, when there is a trump suit. In this case, spades are trumps. After getting rid of two hearts, South will still have one low heart. He will lose one heart trick, but then he can ruff any further hearts that are led.

The principle is clearer if we change the example slightly.

33.
                       North
                       ♠ 4 3 2
                       ♥ 7 6 5
                       ♦ None

West   East

                       South
                     ♠ A K Q J 10
                     ♥ 4 3 2
                     ♦ A K Q

If hearts were led, South would lose three tricks in the suit, as before. Instead, South leads diamonds. North discards the five of hearts on the ace of diamonds, another heart on the king of diamonds, and the last heart on the queen of diamonds.

After these three tricks have been played, North has no more hearts. Now South can lead a low heart from his hand and ruff in the dummy! The discards have paved the way for ruffing tricks.

13. Planning
A Complete Hand

At the beginning of your bridge career each trick seems to stand by itself. Gradually you will get used to the various devices that produce tricks or establish suits, and you will then be able to think of several tricks that are related to one another.

The day will eventually come when you are able to see the thirteen tricks as a related whole. Don't be discouraged if that day takes a long time to come. Many bridge players never plan a hand properly, but they continue to play the game with great enjoyment!

You are not yet ready, of course, to plan the entire play of a hand, but you should expect to do so eventually. You will reach the goal sooner than you expect if you start with a few fundamental principles for playing at notrump and suit bids.

THE PLAY AT NOTRUMP

When you play a hand at a notrump contract, count the tricks that your hand plus the dummy can win in top cards. Compare that total with the number of tricks that you need for your contract.

If you can make your contract with these tricks that you can take "on the run," do so and get on to the next hand. If you find that you cannot make your contract with top cards alone, look for some reasonable way to develop the additional tricks that you need.

34.

North
- ♠ 7 4
- ♥ K 4 2
- ♦ K 7 4
- ♣ Q J 10 9 2

West
- ♠ Q J 10 9 8 2
- ♥ 9 3
- ♦ 10 8 2
- ♣ A 6

East
- ♠ 6 5
- ♥ Q J 10 8
- ♦ Q J 9 5
- ♣ 8 4 3

South
- ♠ A K 3
- ♥ A 7 6 5
- ♦ A 6 3
- ♣ K 7 5

The bidding:

South	West	North	East
1 NT	Pass	2 NT	Pass
3 NT	Pass	Pass	Pass

First, see how the bidding tallies with what you have learned. South has a count of 18 points with balanced distribution and a stopper in each suit. He has a model opening bid of one notrump.

North has a count of 9 points in high cards and balanced distribution. Hence he can afford to raise to two notrump.

South proceeds on to game (three notrump) because he has better than the bare minimum of 16 points. He knows that North will provide 8 or 9 points, and that his own 18 points will then make the combined total either 26 or 27 points.

West "opens" the queen of spades after the final pass by East. That is, West's first lead is the queen of spades. The first lead of any hand is usually called the "opening lead." (Incidentally, West is hoping to establish his own spade suit!)

Now the dummy is put down on the table. You are South, the declarer. How do you plan to play the hand?

Don't be in a hurry to play the first card from the dummy. Nobody will give you a prize for playing quickly from the dummy—or even for playing the whole hand quickly. It's true that nobody will thank you for wasting time either, but you're entitled to a brief moment for thought.

First thought: How many tricks can you win in top cards? The answer is six. You can, if you choose, rattle off the first six tricks by taking in succession the ace and king of spades, the ace and king of hearts, and the ace and king of diamonds. But then your immediate tricks come to an end.

Second thought: How many additional tricks do you need for your contract? The answer is three.

Third thought: How can you develop the additional tricks that you need for your contract?

This is the important part of your planning. You won't always find an easy way to develop the tricks that you need, but in this particular hand the way is fairly clear.

Nothing much can be done with spades, hearts, or diamonds. You will be able to take your six tricks in top cards, of course, but you won't find any additional tricks in those suits.

The three tricks can be found easily, however, in clubs. The opponents must be given their ace of clubs, but then you will be able to win the rest of the tricks in the suit.

Your first step, after making this plan, is to win the first trick with the king of spades. Then you develop your club tricks by leading the king of clubs from your hand.

Notice that you don't begin by taking your six tricks in top cards. The general rule is to *develop your additional tricks first, and to take the top tricks later*. We'll come back to this rule in a moment and show you the reason for it.

When you lead your king of clubs, West takes the trick with the ace of clubs, and he returns the jack of spades, his long suit.

You win this trick with the ace of spades, and now you intend to take your tricks!

You lead a club from your own hand (South) and win the trick with dummy's queen. Dummy now leads the jack of clubs, winning the trick.

To make a long story short, dummy can continue to lead clubs, winning each trick. In all, dummy wins four club tricks—with the queen, jack, ten, and nine. (On the ten of clubs and on the nine of clubs South must discard—and South can easily spare a low heart and a low diamond.)

You have now won two spade tricks and four clubs. That makes six tricks, and you still have the ace and king of hearts and the ace and king of diamonds. You win four tricks with those cards, thus taking a total of ten tricks. That is one trick more than you need for your contract.

Now that you've made your contract, let's go back to the reason for not "cashing" your top tricks at the beginning of the play. If you did, you would win only those six tricks instead of the ten tricks that you managed to win by the proper line of play!

Lay out the cards again and see how the play goes. West leads the queen of spades, and you win with the king. You then win another trick with the ace of spades, and you continue to win tricks in succession with the ace and king of hearts, and the ace and king of diamonds.

Now you lead the king of clubs. West promptly takes his ace of clubs, winning the trick.

West can now lead the jack of spades, winning the trick. He follows with the ten of spades, winning that trick also. And he continues with two more spade tricks.

When West has finished with the spades he leads a diamond. This card is won by East's queen of diamonds. East then leads the jack of diamonds, which wins the thirteenth trick.

If you have played the cards out carefully, you know that the defenders have taken seven tricks to your six. You have thrown away four tricks by taking your top cards in a hurry!

After you have won the first trick with the king of spades, the ace of spades is the most precious card in your hand. It is a "stopper," because it will enable you to *stop* West from running his long spade suit.

The ace of clubs serves as a stopper for the defenders. You cannot win club tricks until you have driven out their ace of clubs, but they cannot win spade tricks until they have driven out your king and ace of spades.

A stopper is like a door that you can shut in the face of the enemy. If you waste a stopper by using it up too early when you are not forced to do so, you are deliberately opening the door to the enemy.

Now think back to what you were told about stoppers in the section on bidding notrump. In general, you were advised to have stoppers in at least three suits (and all four suits when possible) for any notrump bid. This advice, like all reasonable bidding advice, is based on the needs of the play.

THE PLAY AT A SUIT CONTRACT

When you play a hand at a trump contract, count the number of tricks that you *expect to lose*. Compare that total with the number of tricks that you can *afford to lose*.

If you can well afford to give up the losing tricks that you have counted, and still make your contract, play the hand quickly and get on to the next one. If you find that you cannot afford to lose all of those tricks, you must look for a way to eliminate some of the losers.

As you have seen, you can eliminate losing tricks by either discarding them on a long suit, or by ruffing them. These two devices call for two different methods of playing the hand:

When you want to discard losers, draw trumps.

When you want to develop ruffing tricks, don't draw trumps.

The difference is illustrated in the examples that follow:

35.
                          North
                          ♠ 7 6 3
                          ♥ K 7 6
                          ♦ K 8 5
                          ♣ Q J 10 9

West   East
♠ Q J 10 9 2   ♠ K 8 4
♥ 10 5 2   ♥ 9 3
♦ 4 2   ♦ Q J 10 9
♣ 8 7 5   ♣ A 6 3 2

                          South
                          ♠ A 5
                          ♥ A Q J 8 4
                          ♦ A 7 6 3
                          ♣ K 4

The bidding:

South	West	North	East
1 ♥	Pass	2 ♥	Pass
4 ♥	Pass	Pass	Pass

Notice that the bidding conforms to what you have been taught in the first part of this book. South has a count of 20 points (18 points in high cards and 2 points for the doubletons). He opens the bidding in his long heart suit. North raises to two hearts with a total of 9 points in high cards, including proper trump support for the heart suit.

South now adds a point for his fifth heart, bringing the value of his hand up to 21 points. South can therefore well afford to proceed on to game in hearts.

West's opening lead is the queen of spades, and South should plan the play of the hand before he plays even the first card from the dummy. The plan begins with a count of losers.

South must expect to lose one trick in spades. His ace will take one spade trick, but then his other spade is worthless. There is no loser in the trump suit, since South has all of the high cards in the suit between his own hand and the dummy. South may lose two diamond tricks since there are four diamonds in his hand, and only the ace and the king can be depended upon to win tricks. South must lose a club trick to the ace, but after that dummy's clubs will be established.

On the basis of this first count South sees four losers—one in spades, two in diamonds, and one in clubs. South now looks for a way to develop ruffing tricks, or discards, or both.

Dummy has no short suit, and no ruffing tricks can therefore be developed. As a general rule, you look for chances to ruff in the *dummy,* not in your own hand.

South must therefore look for discards. He sees that dummy's clubs can be established, and that it will then be possible to discard losers on dummy's clubs.

South can now proceed to play the hand. His general campaign is to obtain discards on dummy's clubs. Hence, South must plan to draw trumps early.

South wins the first trick with the ace of spades, and leads a low trump to dummy's king. In beginning the trump suit, the first trump is won in the short hand.

Dummy wins the first trump trick with the king and leads another trump. South wins the second trump with the ace and promptly leads a third round of trumps by leading the queen of hearts. After three rounds of trumps have been led, neither East nor West has a trump left. The defenders have been obliged to follow suit on each round, and therefore their trumps have been "drawn."

Now we can see why South must draw trumps. South wants to lead out a number of club tricks. He does not want an oppo nent to win one of these club tricks by ruffing with a small trump. South therefore draws all of the trumps held by the enemy.

Having done so, South should now leave the trump suit alone. He has counted the thirteen cards of the trump suit, and knows that the two trumps still in his hand are the twelfth and thirteenth cards of the suit.

South next begins to establish the clubs by leading the king of clubs from his own hand. As always, the suit is developed by leading a high card from the short hand.

East takes the ace of clubs and thereby gains the right to lead to the next trick. East then leads the king of spades, winning the trick. When East continues with another spade, South can ruff.

The normal value of a *long* trump suit is that each trump acts as a stopper. At notrump, as we have seen, you can stop the enemy's long suit only if you can win a trick in the suit itself. At a trump contract you can stop the enemy's long suit by ruffing when you run out of their suit.

After ruffing the spade, South is in position to go back to the clubs. He leads his low club to dummy's queen, thus enabling the dummy to continue with the jack of clubs and then with the ten of clubs. Each of these clubs wins a trick, and South is able to discard two low diamonds on the jack and ten of clubs.

Having discarded two losers, South easily wins the rest of the tricks with the ace and king of diamonds and the last trump. South therefore makes eleven tricks, one more than he needed for his contract.

Some features of the play of this hand resemble the play of the notrump hand (No. 34). As in that hand, South does not hurry to lead out his winning cards. He wins the first spade trick and then draws three rounds of trumps, but he does not draw any extra trumps, nor does he lead out the ace or king of diamonds.

As in the case of the notrump hand, the high cards can wait. *South must do his suit establishment first and take his high cards later on.* This is the general rule for trump contracts exactly as it was for notrump contracts.

The rule is based on good common sense, just like all the

rules of bridge that you are expected to follow. If South leads out all of his trumps, or if he takes the ace and king of diamonds too early he will lose his game contract.

Let's see what happens if South takes *all* of his trumps before he begins the clubs. When South then leads the king of clubs, East will take the ace of clubs. East will then lead the king of spades, winning the trick. He will continue with another spade, and South will be unable to stop the suit because he will have no trumps left in his hand. There will be no way to prevent West from winning a trick with each of his remaining spades. In all, the defenders will take four spade tricks and the ace of clubs, thus "setting" the contract two tricks.

South would lose his contract likewise if he drew only three rounds of trumps but then needlessly led out the ace and king of diamonds before establishing the clubs. If South adopted this foolish way of playing the hand, East would take the ace of clubs, win a second trick with the king of spades, and then take two diamond tricks with his queen and jack. The total for the defenders would be four tricks, setting the contract one trick.

36.

North
♠ 7
♥ J 10 9 7
♦ A J 8 6 4
♣ 7 4 3

West
♠ K Q 10 9 2
♥ 5 2
♦ 7 3
♣ A Q 9 2

East
♠ 8 6 5
♥ 4 3
♦ K Q 10 9 5
♣ J 10 6

South
♠ A J 4 3
♥ A K Q 8 6
♦ 2
♣ K 8 5

The bidding:

South	West	North	East
1 ♥	1 ♠	2 ♥	Pass
4 ♥	Pass	Pass	Pass

South has a sound opening bid of one heart, with a count of 19 points (17 points in high cards, and 2 points for the singleton). West has a sound overcall of one spade, since he can expect to win about three or four tricks in spades and about two tricks in clubs. North has a good raise to two hearts, since he has good support for hearts with a count of 6 points in high cards and 2 points for the singleton.

After North's raise, South adds one point for the value of his fifth heart. His count is now 20 points, and he expects North to have about 8 points for the raise. Hence there should be a play for game with a total in the combined hands of 28 points.

West should not bid again. He can expect to win only five or six tricks, and may therefore run into a bad penalty if he bids as high as four spades.

West opens the king of spades, and South plans the play as dummy goes down. The plan begins with a count of losing tricks.

South counts three losing cards in spades, since only the ace can be expected to win a trick. There are no losers in trumps. South need not worry about losing a diamond, since he has only one, and dummy's ace will take care of that. In clubs South must expect to lose at least two tricks, and possibly all three.

On the basis of this first count South must expect to lose three spades, and perhaps three clubs. This is a total of six tricks, which is far more than South can afford to lose.

What plan can be adopted to eliminate some of the losers? South can expect to *ruff his losing spades in the dummy*. Since this is the basis of the plan, South *does not draw trumps*.

South wins the first trick with the ace of spades and immediately returns a spade to ruff it in the dummy.

Now South wants to return to his own hand several times, each time to lead a spade and ruff it in the dummy. The easiest way to get back and forth, as required, is to ruff diamonds in the South hand and to ruff spades in the North hand. This type of play is known as a "crossruff."

South therefore continues by leading out dummy's ace of diamonds. He then leads another diamond from dummy and ruffs it in his own hand.

This gives South the right to lead again. He leads another spade and ruffs it in the dummy. Now dummy can lead another diamond for South to ruff. And South can then lead his last spade and ruff it in the dummy.

South will eventually lose all three club tricks, but he will still make his contract.

14. Defensive Play

Defensive play is the most difficult department of contract bridge. When you are declarer you can see your partner's hand (the dummy) and plan the play of your combined resources. When you are a defender, however, you don't see your partner's hand and must therefore plan the play "in the dark."

This doesn't mean that you just play any card on a hit-or-miss basis. You must still plan your play, but you have less evidence to help you make your plan.

DEFENDING AGAINST NOTRUMP: As a general rule you must develop a long suit to defeat a notrump contract. The opening lead should be made in a long suit, and it is usually wise to keep hammering away at that suit whenever you or your partner win a trick later on. Don't keep switching from one suit to another when you have your chances to lead against a notrump contract.

DEFENDING AGAINST A SUIT CONTRACT: It isn't necessary to develop a long suit when you are defending against a suit contract. Avoid leading a suit that gives declarer a chance to take a successful finesse. Prefer to lead suits in which your side has two or three *high cards;* you can't expect to develop tricks out of *low* cards. Don't lead a suit that dummy can ruff.

GENERAL RULES AGAINST ANY CONTRACT: When in doubt about the right suit to lead, look at the dummy. When the dummy is at your left, lead a suit in which dummy has "broken strength." (The ace-king-queen or king-queen-jack is "solid strength," but the ace-queen or king-jack would be "broken strength.")

When the dummy is at your right, lead a suit in which dummy is weak. This is known as leading "up to weakness." Such a lead gives your partner a chance to take a finesse after declarer has already played.

SECOND HAND PLAYS: When you are the second person to play to a trick your play depends on whether a high card or a low card has been led. If a low card has been led, you should usually play a low card from your own hand. This is the basis of the old saying: "Second hand low." If a high card is led, however, it is usually wise to play a winning card (if you have such a card in your hand) or a higher card than the card led even if you cannot win the trick. (However, do not "cover" an honor that is led from the dummy if dummy also has the next highest honor, in sequence with the card that has been led.)

THIRD HAND PLAYS: When only low cards have been played, win the trick if you can. If you cannot play a winning card, play a high card. However, play only as high as necessary to win the trick or force out a higher card.

For example, suppose you hold king-queen-deuce of the suit that has been led. Your partner has led a small card and dummy has played a small card. It is up to you to play the third card on the trick; or, in bridge language, you are "third hand." Your correct play is the *queen*. This is one of your high cards, because you must play high rather than low. However, the queen is the most economical card that will do the job of playing high.

FOURTH HAND PLAYS: When you are last to play to a trick, win the trick if you can—provided, of course, that your partner has not already played a winning card. If you win a trick, win with the cheapest possible card.

FINESSING OVER THE DUMMY: When the dummy is at your right, you may have the chance to take a finesse on a second-hand or third-hand play. For example:

37.

North (dummy)
♠ A Q 10
♥ Q 9 8

West
♠ 9 8 7 6
♥ 7 6 5 4

East
♠ K J 5
♥ K J 10

South
♠ 4 3 2
♥ A 3 2

You are East, defending against some contract (either suit or notrump) played by South. The North hand is the dummy, and you are in position to take finesses behind the dummy.

Suppose your partner, West, leads a heart. Dummy plays the eight of hearts, and it is up to you to play next. Your correct play is the ten. This finesses against dummy's queen, and you know that the finesse will succeed. South must either play the ace or allow your ten of hearts to win the trick.

Notice that this play will prevent dummy's queen of hearts from winning a trick. If you make the mistake of playing the king of hearts, however, South will play the ace of hearts to capture your king; and then dummy's queen will be established.

Similarly, if spades are led, you will be able to play behind (after) the dummy. If dummy plays the ten, you can win with the jack of spades; and if dummy plays the queen, you can win with the king of spades.

DEFENSIVE SIGNALS

Every play that you make is a signal of some kind. If you lead a suit, you probably have some hope of developing a trick in the suit, for example. If you fail to win a trick fourth hand, your partner can probably assume that you didn't have a card high enough to win. This sort of information is always available to the player who takes the trouble to think.

There are also a few special defensive signals that will help you inform your partner on defense. Try to make them part of your bridge knowledge, and look for them when your partner likewise uses them. A signal flashed by one partner is worthless if the other partner fails to recognize it.

The most important defensive signal is the "high-low." This consists of playing a higher card than necessary when you are just following suit and when you are not trying to win the trick; you follow up by playing a lower card at the next trick.

For example, suppose your partner leads the king of spades and you follow suit with the nine of spades. Your partner wins the first trick and promptly leads the ace of spades, on which you play the three of spades. You have played the nine of spades first and the three of spades next — a high-low.

The meaning of a high-low is: "Partner, lead this suit again." Your partner may not know your reason, but he should do as you ask. Perhaps you have the queen of spades and hope to win the third trick with it; or perhaps you have only two spades and hope to ruff the third round of spades.

The opposite of the high-low is the low-high. This means: "Partner, I have no special wish for you to continue with this suit." Your partner may still lead the suit a third time, but only if he has a good reason of his own to do so.

Both signals may be used when you are discarding as well as when you are following suit. When you make your discard play a high card from your strong suit. This tells your partner that you have strength in that suit. If you discard a low card, you tell your partner that you have no particular strength in that suit.

Avoid a discarding signal that may weaken your holding in the suit. In other words, don't throw away a card that may win a trick just to tell your partner where your strength is. Signal strength only if it is urgent that your partner know exactly where your strength is. When it is not so urgent, just make normal plays and let your partner get a pleasant surprise to find you winning tricks where he didn't expect them.

THE OPENING LEAD

When your partner has bid, lead his suit. The only question is which card of the suit to lead.

With a singleton in his suit, you have no choice; lead the singleton. With a doubleton in partner's suit, lead the higher card. With three or more cards in partner's suit it is usually best to lead your top card in the suit.

When your partner has not bid, you must make a "blind" opening lead. The choice depends on the nature of your hand, on whether the contract is a suit or notrump, and on how high the contract happens to be.

LEADING AGAINST NOTRUMP: In general you open your longest and strongest suit. That is, open your longest suit; and with two suits of equal length, open the stronger suit. If the suit is headed by three cards in sequence, lead the top card. Otherwise, lead the fourth-highest card in the suit.

Suppose you hold K-Q-J-6-4 of a suit. Lead the king. The king, queen, and jack are "in sequence" so you lead the top card.

Suppose you hold Q-J-10-6-4 of a suit. Lead the queen. The queen, jack, and ten are "in sequence" so you lead the top card.

Suppose you hold J-10-9-6-4 of a suit. Lead the jack. The jack, ten, and nine are "in sequence" so you lead the top card.

Suppose you hold K-J-7-5-3 of a suit. Lead the five. The suit is not headed by three honors in sequence, so you count down from the top until you get to the fourth-highest card—which is the card to lead.

Suppose you hold Q-9-7-3-2 of a suit. Lead the three. The suit is not headed by three honors in sequence, so you count down from the top until you get to the fourth-highest card.

LEADING AGAINST A SUIT BID: There is no need to lead a long suit. Your best bet, usually, is to *lead an unbid suit*. The declarer will usually try to develop the suits he and the dummy have bid, so there is no need for you to attack such suits. Your tricks will probably come from the other suits.

If you have a choice among the unbid suits, prefer a suit in which you have a sequence of honors. Lead the king from K-Q-J; the queen, from Q-J-10; or the jack, from J-10-9. It is also correct to lead the king from a suit headed by A-K.

Against a trump contract (but not against notrump) you may lead the higher card of only *two* honors in sequence in an unbid suit. For example, lead the king from a suit headed by K-Q; lead the queen from a suit headed by Q-J.

When you have no sequence of honors in an unbid suit, lead a fourth-best card from an unbid suit in which you have length. However, do not lead low from a suit headed by the ace; lead some other suit.

Occasionally you will get good results by leading a singleton. Your partner may be able to return the suit before trumps have been drawn, and you may be able to ruff away one of declarer's high cards.

Don't be upset if you can't find a desirable opening lead. Some hands are like that. Possibly the contract is unbeatable, no matter what you lead. Possibly you must just guess at the right opening lead, with nothing much to guide you. Sometimes you guess right, and sometimes you guess wrong. Bridge players accept the bad luck with the good.

INDEX

SCORING TABLE

Below the Line

Tricks Over "Book" Bid and Won in	Undoubled	Doubled	Redoubled
Clubs or Diamonds (per trick)	20	40	80
Hearts or Spades (per trick)	30	60	120
Notrump (first trick)	40	80	160
(each later trick)	30	60	120

Game is 100 points or more, scored below the line.

Scores below the line are the same whether declarer is vulnerable or not vulnerable.

Above the Line

Overtricks	Not Vulnerable	Vulnerable
Undoubled	20 points per trick for Clubs or Diamonds; 30 points per trick for Hearts, Spades, or notrump.	
Doubled (per overtrick)	100	200
Redoubled (per overtrick)	200	400
For Making a Doubled or a Redoubled Contract	50	50

SCORING TABLE

Above the Line

UNDERTRICKS (Penalty for being Defeated)	Not Vulnerable	Vulnerable
Undoubled (per undertrick)	50	100
Doubled (first undertrick)	100	200
(each later undertrick)	200	300
Redoubled (first undertrick)	200	400
(each later undertrick)	400	600

Bonuses

HONORS IN ONE HAND

All five honors at a suit; all four aces at notrump	150
Four honors at a suit contract	100

	Not Vulnerable	Vulnerable
SMALL SLAM bid and made	500	750
GRAND SLAM bid and made	1000	1500

RUBBER BONUS

When opponents fail to win a game during the rubber	700
When opponents win a game during the rubber	500

UNFINISHED RUBBER

For one game	300
For a part score in an unfinished game	50